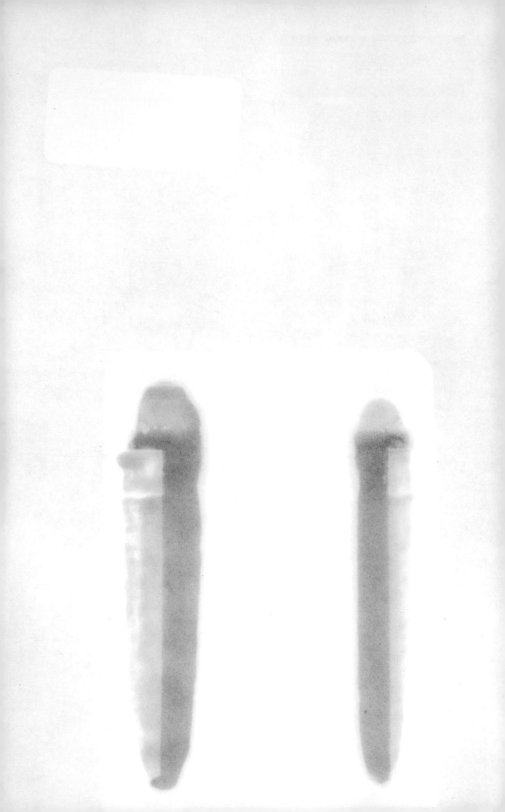

THE MAKING
OF
LLOYD GEORGE

THE MAKING

OF

LLOYD GEORGE

W. R. P. GEORGE

ARCHON BOOKS
1976

First published in 1976
by Faber and Faber Limited
3 Queen Square London WC1
and
in the United States of America
as an Archon Book, an
imprint of The Shoe String Press, Inc.
Hamden, Connecticut 06514

Library of Congress Catalog Card No. 76-022843
ISBN 0-208-01627-9

Printed in Great Britain

CONTENTS

7

ILLUSTRATIONS

AUTHOR'S NOTE

My father William George, David Lloyd George's younger and only brother, died in January 1967 at the age of 101. Some years before his death he had given me a great collection of family papers. As I was working my way through this material I realized its importance in revealing Lloyd George's origins and early aspirations. Reading his early notes and letters, some of which were written in Welsh, it became more apparent to me than ever before how the rural, nonconformist Welsh background from which he sprang had influenced his career. The tide of popular radicalism was rising in Wales during the last thirty years of the nineteenth century; it was taken by Lloyd George at the flood and led on to his political fame and fortune. Nevertheless he himself was not captured by the fervent nonconformity which dominated the Welsh scene during his youth. In fact he was appalled by the sectarianism which reserved salvation to an exclusive body of chosen believers. He felt that he was a victim of this sectarianism, particularly when he was courting Margaret Owen, the daughter of a prominent Methodist deacon. He believed in Christianity as a religion which was to bring life more abundantly to all mankind. Although he inwardly rebelled against the constraints of his Puritan upbringing, he soon found that he had to pay the price of conformity in the eyes of his contemporaries, if he were to succeed in obtaining popular support.

In 1909–10 a considerable quantity of these early family papers was made available to Herbert du Parcq, then a young barrister who subsequently became an eminent judge and a Lord of Appeal in Ordinary. Drawing almost entirely on these early papers he wrote a four-volume biography of Lloyd George before returning them to my father. Almost every subsequent Lloyd George biographer, when writing of the early period, has relied on the original diary entries, letters and notes quoted at length in du Parcq's volumes; but du Parcq was under a disadvantage in that he had no knowledge of the Welsh language and was unfamiliar with the Welsh background which was a dominant influence in the formation of Lloyd George's personality. Du Parcq was only able to quote such extracts from these early letters and diaries as met with my uncle's approval. He did not have access to my father's shorthand diaries nor to other earlier material relating to my grand-father, also called William George, who died when David was only eighteen months old. As a result the published accounts of Lloyd George's origins and youth based on the du Parcq volumes have tended to be incomplete and one-sided.

Over fifty books centring on Lloyd George have appeared since du Parcq's biography, and a reviewer of one of the most recent books remarked that the recording angel would be suffering from writer's cramp before the final and definitive biography appeared some time in the future! The light shed on my uncle's background and youth by original sources, to which I have unrestricted access, is what distinguishes this book from all previous books with a Lloyd George theme. The narrative account of his background and youth finishes when he was first elected to Parliament and entered the wider sphere of British politics in 1890. It was as if at this moment he had suddenly emerged from the chrysalis which until then had confined him.

May 1975   W. R. P. George

ACKNOWLEDGEMENTS

I acknowledge gratefully the permission I have received to quote from the original notes, letters and diaries of David Lloyd George, the copyright of which is now vested in the National Library of Wales and the First Beaverbrook Foundation. I also thank my cousin Lady Olwen Carey-Evans, D.B.E. and her son Mr. D. L. Carey-Evans for their encouragement and assistance. Except where otherwise stated in a footnote I have quoted from original material in my own collection of papers.

I should like to thank Mr. David Jenkins, Librarian of the National Library of Wales, Mr. B. G. Owens, Keeper of Manuscripts and Records at the National Library for their assistance in my research, and Mr. A. J. P. Taylor, F.B.A., Honorary Director of the Beaverbrook Library, for his valuable advice and information in the early stages of writing this book. My friend Dr. Colin Gresham of Criccieth read the first two chapters of the book in typescript and I am grateful to him for several helpful suggestions. My father's and uncle's shorthand diary entries were transcribed by Mr. Stanley Evans of Porthmadog and Mr. G. J. Evans of Penygroes, and I was extremely fortunate that two experts with knowledge of late nineteenth-century shorthand lived near me. Mrs. Mary Jones of Porthmadog helped me with the typing and I am grateful to her.

My publisher, Mr. Charles Monteith, has invariably given me valuable advice and I am greatly indebted to Mrs. Elizabeth Renwick for her careful scrutiny of the typescript and detailed suggestions, most of which I adopted.

Finally I wish to thank Mr. M. E. Starling of Porthmadog for his assistance in preparing the illustrations for the book, and to thank Lady Olwen Carey-Evans for permission to reproduce the early photograph of her mother Margaret, and to thank Mrs. Myfanwy Morris of Porthmadog for permission to reproduce the photograph of Randall Casson, and to thank the Reverend Gomer Roberts, Miss Rhiannon Jones, my cousins Mr. W. J. Phillipps Williams and Mr. J. F. M. Williams, and the Gwynedd Archives Department for helpful information.

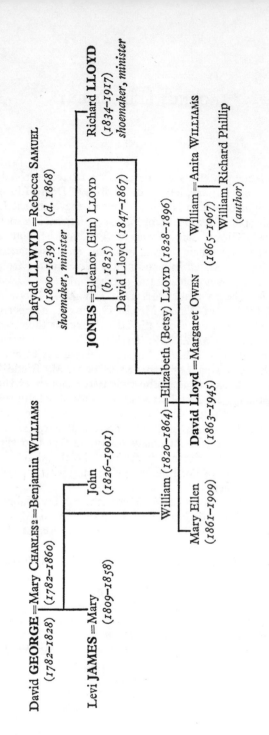

CHAPTER ONE

THE FAMILY

A much-quoted reference to David Lloyd George is a question posed by J. M. Keynes:

How can I convey to the reader, who does not know him, any just impression of this extraordinary figure of our time, this syren, this goat-footed bard, this half-human visitor to our age from the hag-ridden magic and enchanted woods of Celtic antiquity?

Anyone who heard Lloyd George, the elder statesman, entertaining his guests at Churt would agree that he was one of the best story-tellers in the world. He had a mesmeric influence on those who were present, apparently comparable, in Keynes's opinion, to King Arthur holding court; but it is not in the *Mabinogion* that the eloquence and power of Lloyd George have their root and explanation; a just impression of him can only be formed from a knowledge of the family and social background from which he sprang, and the way in which he reacted to that background as its essential qualities became clear to him. His family history reflects the social history of Wales in the latter part of the eighteenth and the first half of the nineteenth century. During his lifetime and since his death in 1945 a great deal has been written about David Lloyd George, but his background has been comparatively neglected. While dealing with his boyhood in the village of Llanystumdwy, for example, writers have noted that his family were the only Baptists in the village, but the significance of this has not been fully realized.

Lloyd George's maternal ancestors, for at least two generations in the Llanystumdwy district, had been Scotch Baptists, a break-away sect from the orthodox Baptists. The sect had been formed as a protest against the laxity, especially in the matter of scriptural interpretation, which, it was said, had overtaken the more ortho-dox nonconformists, be they Methodists or Baptists. The Scotch Baptists represented Protestantism in its extremist form; but their extreme beliefs were devoid of any political content.

The contrast between Lloyd George's origins on the two sides of his family is striking. His mother's family, the Lloyds of Llanystumdwy, realized that they belonged to an extremely small

15

religious sect and that their conduct was under the constant surveillance of their fellow villagers. Contemporary records show that
the Lloyds' evangelical religious zeal inculcated into the younger
members of the family a sturdy independence of outlook combined with an obsessive belief in hard work, self-discipline and
self-help. They did not look to the government of the day for any
assistance beyond the protection of life and property, the preserva-
tion of law and order. They shared the views of a leading Welsh
nonconformist who said that a man could do more for himself at
home and within fifty yards of his own doorstep than Robert Peel
and his cabinet could ever achieve on his behalf. Accordingly they
did not join in the campaign for the extension of popular education. It was a man's duty, according to the number of his talents
given him by God, to educate himself if he wished to do so,
urged on by his own individual conscience and ambition.

The Georges of Pembrokeshire, Lloyd George's paternal
ancestors, were farmers, and several of them owned their own
farms. They were orthodox Baptists in an area where the Baptists
were in a majority compared with the other religious denominations. William George, Lloyd George's father, was a prisoner of
neither his own nor his family's past. His father died when William
was only four. His mother remarried and he left his stepfather's
home to make his own way in the world when he was in his teens.
He left Pembrokeshire soon after to become a schoolmaster and
moved from one post to another without settling down anywhere
for any length of time. In the late 1850s his wanderings brought
him to Pwllheli, where he met and married Elizabeth Lloyd in
1859. He came to live for two years with the Lloyds at Highgate,
the small Llanystumdwy cottage of which they were the tenants.
He brought with him not only many books, but also an outlook on
life and religion which did not accept the limitations imposed by
the tenets of the Scotch Baptists. He discussed politics, for instance, with his brother-in-law, Richard Lloyd, who was destined
to be the guardian and mentor of the young Lloyd George. Richard
Lloyd's father, Dafydd Llwyd, had died at the age of thirty-nine
in 1839, and until he met William George in 1859, Richard Lloyd
would undoubtedly have accepted his father's view, preserved by
his widowed mother Rebecca, that a true Christian leaves political
agitation exclusively to the politicians.

William George was a schoolmaster in Manchester when Lloyd
George was born on 17 January 1863. He was always dogged by
ill-health and a hypersensitive conscience and shortly after Lloyd
George's birth in a final attempt to restore his failing health he gave
up teaching and returned to Pembrokeshire to farm a smallholding.

But he died in June 1864, leaving his wife Elizabeth stranded in south Pembrokeshire with two young children, Mary and David, and to add to her problems she found that she had become pregnant a month or so before her husband's death. This child, my father William George, was born at Llanystumdwy in February 1865, after the fatherless family had been brought there by her brother Richard Lloyd.

William George had probably settled in south Pembrokeshire, a mainly English-speaking county, because his own knowledge of Welsh was very limited. Had he lived his children would have learnt very little, if any, Welsh there, and had he been restored to health he would probably have returned to England to resume his teaching career. As it was his children Mary, David and William, were brought up in the village of Llanystumdwy, a thoroughly Welsh-speaking district, by their mother and bachelor uncle, Richard Lloyd. They were members of the small community of the Disciples of Christ (successors to the Scotch Baptists), whose chapel was at Capel Ucha, Criccieth, about two miles from Llanystumdwy. The children were reared in an extremely strict Puritan climate, but they realized as they grew up that an attribute of the particular sect to which their mother and uncle belonged was a love of religious liberty and the freedom to worship in accordance with the practice of their small, independent denomination, unhampered by the surveillance of any external organization. I believe that one effect on the young Lloyd George of this strictly Puritan upbringing was to transform this influence into a passion for political independence, unhampered as far as possible by a rigid adherence to a party line.

Elizabeth George's father, Dafydd Llwyd, was a shoemaker but, more important to him, he was also unpaid pastor of Capel Ucha, Criccieth. He was ordained in 1830 and has recorded a full account of the service and sermon in two letters he sent to John Salusbury, a Denbighshire minister of the same denomination. He had expected his friend to be present and was bitterly disappointed he had not come. Not only did Salusbury fail to put in an appearance, he also neglected to write and explain his absence. Dafydd Llwyd, writing in Welsh as he invariably did—he probably knew little, if any English—in June 1830, addressed Salusbury as his dear brother and companion in Christ's Gospel. He went on:

I have been waiting, aye, watching for a long time with a keen eye for your letter as promised, but all in vain, like so many other expectations in this disappointing life. As you had promised so definitely to be with us on this occasion, you must know that we had taken it for a

17

certainty you would have been present, if you were in good health. However, the time came, but Salusbury didn't.

I have heard recently, dear Brother, that you have been in Wrexham Fair, telling them that the *world* was too much with them with its cares and troubles; perhaps that was the cause of your absence, but you could have at least written to explain yourself and to wish me well. I have heard that a similar and solemn day has also overtaken you. May the great Head of the Church and the Kingdom's great King give to you of his spirit to be an honest and faithful servant in his work until the end of your days, for accursed is he who is deceitful in the Lord's work, and blessed the good and faithful servant, who deals justly with his Master's property, for he will enter joyfully into the Lord's kingdom. And O! What a wonderful happiness awaits him—what a wonderful privilege will be his prerogative.

He then described his ordination service, and how he was escorted from the congregation by the Elders before being ordained by the imposition of hands by the brethren. He gave Salusbury an account of his elated feelings when Robert Jones preached the ordination sermon and said the effect of the sermon on him was so great that he considered that it should be 'inscribed on the rock for ever by an iron pen'. Finally, he mentioned two young sailors from Criccieth who had been attending services in the Scotch Baptist church in Glasgow on two successive Sundays:

They received a great and warm-hearted welcome and the most loving companionship that Christian brethren could bestow on each other. The Church there has about 70 members. . . . The Elders complained that there was so little correspondence between them and their brethren in Wales. They said these two sailors were the only Welsh brethren they had ever met. On this occasion in their Love Feast [*Cariad Wledd*]* one of the Scotch brethren read the first letters which had passed between John R. Jones and Archibald McLean. D. Williams, one of the two sailors, bought a first edition of McLean's works, consisting of six volumes in all, and he has given them to me. The time has come, dear Brother, to close this letter—you can see that

---

* The Baptists gathering at Capel Ucha, Criccieth in Dafydd Llwyd's days were known as the bread-and-cheese Baptists (*Batis bara-a-chaws*). What John R. Jones and his followers meant by love feast was a homely meal of bread and cheese between the services. Most of the members travelled on foot or horseback many miles to attend the chapel on Sundays and could not get home between the services. It appears that the same practice was followed in the Glasgow church.

I have run out of paper to write on; besides it is now 4 o'clock in the morning and sleep has caught up with me.

I am—

thy Dafydd Llwyd.

Salusbury must have replied to this letter fairly soon after he received it, for Llwyd, writing to him again in December, says he had allowed five months to pass after receiving Salusbury's valuable reply to his first letter. Salusbury had asked for a full note of the ordination sermon preached by Robert Jones, and Llwyd when writing this second letter had still not got over his disappointment at Salusbury's absence:

You know how easily *suspicions* are aroused in our corrupt hearts. . . . But the sight of the hand-writing on the envelope which contained your letter was enough to send them away instantly; these fiery suspicions were but chaff before the strong wind of brotherly love, when once I had opened and read your letter, which brought me great joy.

The correspondence between Dafydd Llwyd and John Salusbury continued for some years, Salusbury having vowed that he would never again make any firm promises. He gave some interesting statistics of the membership of the Scotch Baptist churches in North Wales at Dafydd Llwyd's request:

Rhuthun 6; Llanufydd 25; Llanfairtalhaiarn 36; Llaneilian 12—The cause in Rhuthun was once quite popular and numerous for some time after the secession [presumably from the orthodox Baptists] but consumption soon took the place of the congregation. Death was the principal cause of reducing their number and depriving them of their status as a church and the privileges of belonging to a church; to-day they are only a small, bedraggled company of poor people on the verge of starvation.

The membership of the Criccieth Scotch Baptist church remained exceedingly small, and Dafydd Llwyd never had a congregation of more than twenty-five under his care. His sermon notes show that the salvation of their souls was his overriding concern, to the apparent exclusion of all other interests during the last few years of his life.

The John R. Jones, to whom Dafydd Llwyd referred in his letter, was the founder of the Criccieth church. He had written to Archibald McLean of Edinburgh to say that he had been led under the guidance of Holy Providence to read his books:

I translated some parts before the Church, as they cannot understand the English tongue. We agree with every article in them. There is considerable reformation of late among the Particular Baptists in North Wales, especially concerning Church order and manner of worship; our church is the first in this point. We apprehend it high time indeed for the dear people of God to come out of Babilon and separate themselves according to the Christian rule, in order to have unity of spirit. . . .

He was a leader whose influence lasted for generations after his death in 1822. In stanzas composed by an eminent Welsh poet, Robert ap Gwilym Ddu, a vivid description is given of his ministry in South Caernarfonshire and Merioneth over a period of thirty-four years: not able to afford a horse, he went on foot in all sorts of weather facing every kind of hardship in those poverty-stricken times until he collapsed under the stress of his exertions. Jones was born some forty years before Dafydd Llwyd, but he was his mentor; his beliefs and religious practices were to Llwyd and his fellow Baptists the staff of life. Dafydd Llwyd's religion was a way of life, and however short and unrewarding materially his life as a shoemaker was, the spiritual world he inhabited was full of light and moments of surpassing happiness.

In 1820 at about the same time as he started his shoemaking business and before he became pastor, Dafydd Llwyd helped to found a local debating society, Cymreigyddion, which met at Criccieth to discuss and debate religious and other topics. The earliest of his notes for the society is a dissertation on the importance of morality, both for the sake of a man's family and in helping him to succeed in business. In this address he referred to the recent death of George III, and regarded him as an example of morality, who defended the good but would not tolerate evil in any form. He contrasted him with James I, to the latter's detriment. Clearly Dafydd Llwyd, in common with the majority of his fellow countrymen, regarded George III as a champion of the Protestant cause, and his refusal to emancipate the Catholics during his long reign of anti-Jacobitism, was an overriding virtue. It is however, surprising that Dafydd Llwyd went on to say:

O! may his Majesty George IV continue, as he has from his coronation to the present time, to uphold the dignity and worth of the Crown.

As the scandal of George IV's attempt to divorce Queen Caroline at the beginning of his reign had swallowed up every other topic of public interest between June and November 1820, it would have been natural for Dafydd Llwyd to regard George IV as a monarch who was sullying his father's name as a good family man. That Llwyd did not do so shows he accepted without question the

20

political attitude of an older generation of Welsh nonconformist leaders who must have been amongst the most extreme Tories in Britain. Their principal exponent was an influential Calvinistic Methodist minister and author, Thomas Jones of Denbigh. A group of London Welshmen shortly before the turn of the century had accepted many of the progressive ideas stemming from the French Revolution, and one of their number, Jack Jones, was the licensee of the Canterbury Arms at Southwark during the 1790s, where he met Tom Paine and other advanced thinkers. In 1795 Jack Jones published a Welsh tract *Seren dan Gwmwl* (Star under a Cloud), of which thousands of copies were sold and distributed. In this he set forth Tom Paine's belief in the rights of man, and opposed war and the monarchy, which he associated with tyranny. Thomas Jones's answer to this was to publish and distribute throughout Wales at least 10,000 copies of a tract he called *Gair yn ei Amser* (A Word in Time). He defined his basic attitude to the new thoughts and aspirations engendered by the French Revolution in the following declaration:

Whatever were the causes of the French Revolution, the war and the turmoil in this country, I am certain of this—Sin is the root cause of our misfortunes,—so it is pointless to blame the King and the politicians.

The climate of opinion in which Dafydd Llwyd, and evangelical Welshmen like him, moved had been created by Welsh nonconformist leaders of every denomination, of whose attitudes Thomas Jones was typical. Their counterblast to Jack Jones and those who shared his views was wholly effective. The common folk in Wales, *Y werin*, accordingly accepted that any attempt to achieve an egalitarian society by the redistribution of wealth would be short-lived, leaving in its wake worse poverty than they were already experiencing. It was a corollary of this firm social conviction that the common people should respect the King, his officials and all those placed in authority.

Dafydd Llwyd's sermon notes are typical of the religious beliefs of his age; they teach that in the short time that a man spends on earth—and the time was short in those days—he must be convinced of his fall from divine favour in the Garden of Eden and accept that he faced everlasting perdition, unless he were saved by God's grace and Christ's supreme sacrifice on Calvary. They asked: 'What point is there in the potter's clay arguing about his so-called rights?' Questions concerning man's welfare during his brief sojourn on earth were of no significance, when compared with the importance of what happened to him in the world to come; would he spend eternity in Hell or in Heaven? That was the question constantly and passionately posed by Dafydd Llwyd to his small congregation in Capel Ucha.

Thomas Jones died in 1820, but his influence continued in the sermons of two of the most powerful and eloquent orators Wales has ever known—John Elias, a Calvinistic Methodist, and Christmas Evans, a Baptist.

John Elias's declared opinion was that reformers, such as Grey and Brougham, were sending the country speedily towards disaster. He warned a young colleague, Lewis Edwards, who was destined to become a principal of the Methodist College, in Bala, Merioneth, against entering London University, shortly after its foundation at the instigation of Henry Brougham in 1827. He regarded the young university as a godless institution. Fortunately Edwards paid no heed to his advice and became a religious leader of more enlightened outlook, who helped, during fifty years as principal of the college to pave the way for the Liberal revival in the latter half of the nineteenth century in Wales. It was, of course, the flood-tide of this revival which carried Lloyd George and the other Welsh Liberal leaders into political prominence before the turn of the century.

Dafydd Llwyd's debating society continued to hold its fortnightly meetings during the early 1820s. Generally the topics under discussion were connected with morality: 'Who is the greater enemy of the State—the Drunkard or the Deceiver?' 'Who is the more dangerous—the Flatterer or the Slanderer?' (Dafydd Llwyd thought the Slanderer for, he said, if it were possible for one man to possess all the wealth of Great Britain and Europe together with the two Indias, he would still not have enough to buy back his good name once he had lost it.) 'Whose lust is the greater—the Drunkard's for strong drink or the Miser's for wealth?' (The instances given by Dafydd Llwyd of the social havoc caused by drunkenness in the parish of Llanystumdwy show that this topic was far from being of academic interest only.) 'What is better in the Employer's own self-interest—to be stern or kind towards his servants?' (Dafydd Llwyd is very practical in his reasoning; he says the good and efficient servants will always avoid the stern, bitter-tongued master in the hiring fairs, who will thus always have to accept the lazy and inefficient servants, so creating a vicious circle in which the stern master becomes increasingly embittered with his lot!)

At a meeting of the society in November 1823 Dafydd Llwyd read a paper concentrating on the importance of the Welsh people's retaining their language. I will translate enough of this address to

give a fair indication of its content since it shows that Dafydd
Llwyd was more aware than most of his contemporaries of the
dangers which encompassed the Welsh language. He accepted the
general view expressed by the leading Welsh poets of his age that
George IV was an acceptable king and a direct descendant of Owen
Tudor of Anglesey, Henry VII's grandfather. I have read the work
of two of these poets, who were leading members of this same
society and I have failed to find any expression of anxiety in their
work concerning the survival of the Welsh language. Their general
attitude was that a descendant of the Victor in the Battle of Bosworth in 1485 was on the throne and that accordingly all must be
well with the world, particularly in Wales. After all, they argued,
Henry VII, the founder of the Tudor dynasty, was a Welshman,
and had he not, as Henry Richmond, landed with a force of 2,000
men, at Milford Haven early in August 1485? On his march to
Shrewsbury was he not supported by reinforcements from both
North and South Wales, so that by this time he had 8,000 spears?
A new era had opened with Henry's victory over the slain Richard
at Bosworth. For England it meant that the Wars of the Roses had
at last ended; the Welsh believed that the ancient prophecy of their
bards had been fulfilled and that a Welshman had founded a
dynasty which was to rule over England.

Robert ap Gwilym Ddu, the poet to whom I have already referred and one of the best hymn-writers in the Welsh language,
greeted George IV in verse in 1821, shortly after his coronation,
when he was travelling through Wales en route for Ireland. He
points out that almost 300 years had passed since a 'crowned head
had honoured the fair land of Wales' with his presence. He calls
on the men of Arfon to 'crown their kinsman' and says that Owen
Tudor was indeed his true ancestor. 'May he be a Defender of the
Faith, a true son of his father, and may every yard of his possessions remain his for ever.'

Shortly after the accession of Queen Victoria in 1837, Eben
Fardd, another well-known poet living in south Caernarfonshire,
composed an exceedingly long ode on the 'Victory of Bosworth
Field'. He praises the Welsh blood which flowed through the veins
of Queen Victoria and points out that Henry VII had triumphed
where Owain Glyndwr had failed. But the truth is that the Angli-
cization of Wales gained immense momentum during the reigns of
Henry VII, Henry VIII and Queen Victoria. It was Henry VIII
who, in 1535, passed the notorious law that enacted that, 'No
person or persons that use the Welsh speech or language shall have/
or enjoy any Manner, Office or Fees within this Realm of England,
Wales or other the King's Dominion upon pain of forfeiting the

same Office or Fees, unless he or they use and exercise the English speech or Language.' It was during Queen Victoria's reign that a system of education was introduced in Wales which effectively proscribed the Welsh language as a medium of expression. One effect of this was that whereas Dafydd Llwyd always wrote in Welsh and remained Dafydd Llwyd until his death in 1839, his son was called Richard Lloyd (not Rhisiart Llwyd), and Richard wrote his diaries in English rather than Welsh. In fact, Richard Lloyd, as a schoolboy, was struck on the head with a stick for being caught talking Welsh, and remained deaf in one ear for the rest of his life as result of the injury he received for using his native tongue as his natural means of expression. Wales had to wait until the twentieth century was well advanced before the national language received any encouragement by the State. The language and literature of the country depended on the voluntary literary societies and the chapels for their survival, and it is apparent from Dafydd Llwyd's paper that his society was subject to much adverse comment by 1823, apparently intended to prejudice local opinion against the members. He refers to this in his opening sentences as follows:

Many choice fables are being circulated by the detractors of our cause concerning the objects of our fortnightly meetings; some say that our purpose in meeting is to drink beer, to burn tobacco and gossip, etc; others say we meet together because we consider ourselves above our neighbours in wisdom. Both criticisms are unfounded, and if only those who bear false witness against us would listen to the truth and reason, their mouths would be as closely shut as the frog's mouth in the month of July. We never drink more than tuppence worth of beer of a night. Whatever deceit is perpetrated by our critics concerning us, we say without hesitation or one iota of shame that the principal object of our Society is to defend, nourish and to brighten the language of our country, that is the Welsh language. We are proud to declare this.

It is the duty of each nation to defend the use of the native language, even if it were the poorest language. How much greater is our duty to defend the use of the Welsh language, which we are assured by linguists is one of the most glorious languages on earth. It is as much our duty to defend our country against being overcome by a foreign language, as it is to defend our territory against conquest by a foreign power. . . . Fortunately there are no enemies of our country to-day, and we have members of Parliament to debate our cause; we find the English, Scotch and Irish co-operating in matters affecting our welfare, in the same way as we take part as Welsh people in promoting their welfare. Civil servants and military officers are chosen from amongst us in the same way as they are in other countries. Another thing we can boast of is that we have a King sitting on the throne of Britain, through whose every vein Welsh blood is coursing. It's true that the Isle of Britain once belonged to the Brythonic race, but we no longer have any enemies who wish to attack our nation by land. Nevertheless we have many enemies, cruel enemies, who are very much alive, attacking our language, and it behoves us to fight to defend our native tongue. More often than not the Welsh nation itself is the language's worst enemy. It breaks my heart to say so: THE WELSH NATION IS AN ENEMY OF ITS OWN LANGUAGE.

The Welsh people who were ashamed to use and promote their own language were contemptuously referred to as Dick-John-Davids (Dic-Shon-Dafyddion). Dafydd Llwyd ends his paper with a graphic reference to their fate in the parish of Llanystumdwy:

Let us all aim our shells against the Kingdom of the Dic-Shon-Dafyddion, and I believe that before long no descendant of Dic-Shon-Dafydd will be alive from the source of the Dwyfor river in Cwm Pennant to the estuary where the river reaches the open sea, and that this fine river will carry the stinking corpses of the enemies of the language right out to the depths of the sea: but let no one think that in saying this I mean literally the bodies of living men. I mean the rotten elements which possess some men, and I want a strong North wind to blow these right out to sea, so that their oppressive stench will never more threaten the inhabitants of Eifionydd [i.e. the region of Caernarfonshire through which the river Dwyfor flows].

As Dafydd Llwyd rightly discerned there was a real battle to be fought and won in the educational sector and socially, if the Welsh language was to be preserved and developed for modern usage. The cultural tradition of Wales has for over a thousand years found its principal expression through the medium of the Welsh language, but when the educational institutions and schools of modern Wales were in process of erection, the importance of the language was not sufficiently recognized. This led to the divergence of the new education from the cultural tradition of Wales, rooted in its language. My father, William George, became concerned about the fate of the language in the early years of this century, and entered public life primarily with the intention of initiating educational policies which would tend to promote the use of Welsh. As Chairman of the Caernarfonshire Education Committee for thirty-two years, and for some years chairman of the Central Welsh Board, he took a leading part in the unending struggle to promote the facilities for the effective teaching of Welsh and its recognition as the national language. He realized that in modern conditions the nonconformist denominations in Wales, from their inception the language's principal custodians, could no longer without the assistance of the State ensure its survival.

The Baptists, under the leadership of Joseph Harris, who became known in Wales under his bardic name of Gomer, were responsible for the publication in 1814 of the first weekly newspaper in the Welsh language. Gomer died in 1825, but there are references to the newspaper he founded, called *Seren Gomer* in Dafydd Llwyd's papers. Gomer was a Baptist minister in Swansea, and was one of the first in Wales to take a keen interest in the language question, and the threat posed to its survival, particularly in the valleys of South Wales where the early signs of the industrial revolution were becoming manifest. By reflecting Gomer's concern for the survival of the language in the rural seclusion of Llanystumdwy Dafydd Llwyd was many years ahead of his time. Gomer refused to limit his interests to purely sectarian and theological questions, and this attitude continued to be reflected in the pages of *Seren Gomer* after his death. Dafydd Llwyd might well have broadened his interests during the 1830s in a similar manner, and become better known as a leader of thought in south Caernarfonshire, had not the Criccieth Baptist church at Capel Ucha during the 1830s been assailed by yet another sectarian onslaught. This came from the United States and concerned a movement by a group called the Disciples of Christ, of which Alexander Campbell was the principal leader. His views concerning the proper expression and practice of the Christian religion were contained in a tract called *The British Millennial Harbinger.*

Alexander Campbell was born in Scotland but emigrated with his father to America in 1809. His beliefs were, in effect, to simplify yet further the doctrine of McLean, accepted by J. R. Jones, the founder of the Criccieth community of Scotch Baptists, and to bring the church nearer to the unsullied elements of Christianity as expressed in the gospel. One of these was that there was no such office as Minister—all were equal in the sight of God. The followers of Campbell ceased to address Dafydd Llwyd as the Reverend Dafydd Llwyd. The link between the Criccieth church and Alexander Campbell was William Jones of Tremadog whose influence over the unorthodox Baptists in the district had replaced the leadership of J. R. Jones. *The British Millennial Harbinger* was translated into Welsh, and Dafydd Llwyd was told by a fellow Baptist that it contained letters, which were nearest to God's Word as contained in the Bible. William Jones advocated the new doctrine whenever he visited the Criccieth church, but the evidence suggests that Dafydd Llwyd did not accept the Campbellite interpretation of the Gospel in its entirety and kept the Criccieth church from joining the Disciples of Christ during his lifetime. He died in 1839, and the Criccieth church joined the Disciples of Christ denomination in 1841 and remained affiliated to it for over ninety years until the 1930s when it became a member church of the Welsh Baptist Union. During most of Lloyd George's lifetime he was a member of the Disciples of Christ church at Criccieth, of which there had been no paid ministry; unlike all the other nonconformist chapels in the district, the Criccieth chapel of the Disciples of Christ had no *Sêt Fawr* (Deacon's Pew) and no deacons. The doctrine of Alexander Campbell was carried out conscientiously and literally by Richard Lloyd and his fellow members; the extreme simplicity of the service, the complete lack of pomp and ostentation and the reiterated theme that all were equal in the sight of God combined to make an indelible impression on the mind of the young Lloyd George, however much he inwardly rebelled, as he often did, against the constraints of his Puritan upbringing.

The Criccieth church was introduced to the teaching of Alexander Campbell in about 1835 and soon after this Dafydd Llwyd was also afflicted by a physical trial—a persistent stomach ailment. During the week-days he worked hard at his trade as a shoemaker, staying up until the small hours of the morning to prepare his sermons. He would be expected to preach at least twice on Sundays, and the preparation of two new sermons a week was a task which, coupled with writing letters to brethren in other North Wales churches of similar persuasion, robbed him of the sleep he badly needed. He was reputed to have been of a fine physique, and a man who travelled, like J. R. Jones, on foot to attend preaching meetings at considerable distances from home, over roads which were little better than dirt-tracks, pitted with mudfilled potholes whenever it rained. A few months before his death at the age of thirty-nine on 25 October 1839 there is a pathetic hint of Dafydd Llwyd's efforts to regain his health in a letter he received from William Jones. The letter is dated 17 June and is sent in response to Dafydd Llwyd's inquiry concerning some stomach pills. William Jones tells him that he had found the following advertisement after searching through some dozens of copies of *Seren Gomer* (the Welsh Baptist journal):

Morison's Universal Medicines having superseded the use of almost

27

all the patent medicines which the wholesale Vendors have foisted upon the credulity of the searchers after health for so many years, the Town Druggists and Chemists have plunged into the mean expedient of puffing up a Dr. Morrison, a being who never existed, as prescribing Vegetable Universal Pills Nos. 1 & 2 etc. KNOW ALL MEN then that this attempted delusion must fail under the fact that none can be held genuine by the College but those which have impressed upon the box the Government stamp 'Morison's [with one r] Vegetable Universal Medicine'.

He then says he hopes this 'Quack Medicine' will cure Dafydd Llwyd of his ailment, so that he could once more preach as effectively as he had in the past. He seeks to comfort Dafydd Llwyd, as if he realized that this might be a vain hope, by saying that when we travel through 'that valley', our most valuable possession will be the ability to declare with a clear conscience 'I have fought the good fight' and I gather from the letter he was sure Dafydd Llwyd would be able to make that declaration.

Dafydd Llwyd was buried in the small and now disused cemetery adjacent to Capel Ucha, Penymaes in Criccieth, which was the meeting place of the Scotch Baptists to whom he ministered. The church record notes: *Felly y cyfiawn hwn a gymerwyd ymaith megis o ganol drygfyd* [Thus this just man was taken away as if out of the midst of adversity].

The Christian religion was to him the most real and important fact in life, as evidenced by his notebooks and his family Bible—called 'Beibl Peter Williams'—which are now in my possession. His first act on marrying Rebecca Samuel in 1824 was to purchase a copy of the 1823 edition of Peter Williams's Welsh Bible. The first edition of this Bible was published in 1770, and 8,600 copies were sold. On the appropriate blank page of his Bible he carefully noted not only the date but the actual hour of the birth of his three children:

Eleanor our first-born 12 September 1825, about 5.30 Monday morning.

Elizabeth our second daughter 1 October 1828, between 11 and 12 Wednesday morning.

Richard our son 12 July 1834 between noon and one o'clock Saturday afternoon.

His widow Rebecca survived for many years to face the grind of bringing up the three young children and keeping the shoemaking business going to support the family. The summer of 1839 had been wet and uncertain, with a poor harvest. There had been a marked reduction in the incomes of the tenant-farmers and agricultural workers upon whose support the prosperity of the shoemaking business mainly depended. A contemporary poet from the parish of Llanystumdwy remarked that the farm labourer had to share between nine of his children what would have been sufficient for one. Rebecca Llwyd would have known that many mothers with young children like her own had been driven to work on farms for a pittance to keep the family from starving. This was the adversity, referred to in the church record on the death of Dafydd Llwyd, which Rebecca was now left to face depending solely on her own innate resourcefulness and an unshakeable faith in the abiding goodness of God's providence.

CHAPTER TWO

LLANYSTUMDWY

In his address on the Welsh language to the debating society
Dafydd Llwyd referred in admiration to the Dwyfor river which
flows through the parish of Llanystumdwy and the heart of the
village. This river to me is the living link with the past and with
my ancestors. If you come to Llanystumdwy to visit David Lloyd
George's grave, whatever route you take and wherever you come
from, you will arrive at the river. When he accepted an earldom,
knowing he was about to cross another river, it was with the
Dwyfor river he wished his name to be linked. There are two
rivers flowing through the parish of Llanystumdwy, the Dwyfor
and Dwyfach, 'Great Goddess' and 'Little Goddess'. The Dwyfor
was never a formidable or strange goddess to the children of the
village—she was a playful goddess.

Looking downstream through the branches from Lloyd George's
grave, you will get a glimpse of the three-arched grey stone bridge
which spans the Dwyfor. The symmetry of the completed bridge
has a timeless quality, as if it had always been part of the land-
scape, its dominance in the village verifying the old Welsh proverb—'*A fo ben bid bont*' (He who would be head let him be a
bridge). In reality we know that the bridge did not spring fully-
fashioned from the stony and rocky river-bed; we know that it is a
lasting memorial to the craftsmanship of stonemasons and labourers
whose dust is untraceable in the village churchyard. These dedicated and underpaid craftsmen did their work so well that the
County Highway Authority today allows articulated vehicles,
carrying up to thirty-two tons, to cross and re-cross the bridge, a
bridge which was only meant for one horse-drawn cart, waggon or
coach to cross at a time. It is only its narrowness which is compelling the County Highway Authority to construct a by-pass to
the south of the village with a new bridge across the Dwyfor.

Dafydd Llwyd also referred to the Dwyfor having her source in
Cwm Pennant. Cwm Pennant is still largely an undiscovered
valley, which must look today much as it did immediately after the
Ice Age, when a huge glacier shaped like a boomerang had
vanished, leaving a verdant valley to cradle the young Dwyfor. The
placidity of the Dwyfor during her seaward course, as she meanders

30

through arable farmlands and spinneys, is emphasized by slow curves in the river-bed which arrest the flow of water. These near about-turns of the Dwyfor form shaded pools, much sought after by salmon and sea-trout anglers. Each of these pools has its name. For generations the children of Llanystumdwy have been told the names of these pools, although they are not recorded on any Ordnance Survey map: 'Llyn Gwragedd' (The Women's Pool); 'Llyn Meirch' (The Mares' Pool) in Trefan Woods—here the water cascades like the mane of a white mare over the small rocks— there cannot be a more beautiful river-pool this side of Keats's 'faery lands forlorn'. On the seaward side of Llanystumdwy Bridge there is 'Llyn yr Allt Goch' (The Pool of the Red Hill). Did some tribal blood, drawn in a now-forgotten skirmish, redden the silver water of Dwyfor near Yr Allt Goch? The pool where the waters of Dwyfor and Dwyfach meet before entering the anonymity of the sea, is called 'Llyn y Ddwy Afon' (The Pool of the Two Rivers).

When the two rivers, now one, are literally within a hundred yards of the beach and open sea, with only a flimsy barrier of sand and shingle to bar their exit, unaccountably their waters turn sharply towards the east and flow again placidly for a mile on the landward side of the beach before turning abruptly south and suddenly entering the sea, without forming any kind of estuary, as if they said: 'Let us have a quick death!' The name of the village— 'Llanystumdwy'—is derived from this reluctance of the two rivers to enter the sea and to cling as long as possible to the land. As already mentioned, '*Dwy*' is a Celtic goddess; '*Ystum*' is a turn or bend; '*Llan*' is a church, so that we have, translated literally— 'The Church of the Turning of Dwy', a combination of Celtic paganism and traditional Christianity, which may well have moulded the character of the best-known son of that parish— David Lloyd George, or Uncle David, as, of course, I always knew him.

At school in Llanystumdwy the children were not taught Welsh poetry, nor were they introduced to the epic stories recorded in the *Mabinogion*. The young Lloyd George was not told that once upon a time Math son of Mathonwy was lord of Gwynedd, and that he could not live save while his two feet were in the fold of a maiden's lap, unless the turmoil of war prevented him. Math was not only overlord of Gwynedd, but a magician at whose behest the fairest maiden that mortal ever saw was called forth from the flowers of the oak, and the flowers of the broom, and the flowers of the meadowsweet. Math gave this maiden, called *Blodeuwedd* (Choice Flower), in marriage to a young man whom he set in

31

authority over a region which included Eifionydd, the name of the
district where the village of Llanystumdwy is situated.

The children were not told these stories at home either, but
they were told that a wheel of fire was sometimes to be seen at
night careering downhill towards the bridge which crossed the
river Dwyfach in the depth of the woods. This wheel of fire was to
keep the devil away whenever he sought to enter the village of
Llanystumdwy. These woods where the children played and
whiled away their childhood aroused in them a sense of kinship
with an earlier and more primitive age. At that time the beeches
and oak trees were older and more magnificent around Llanystumdwy than in any other part of Gwynedd; and although many
of the older trees were felled during the First World War, and the
pick of the centuries-old beeches more recently, Llanystumdwy
still retains its predominantly sylvan character. The ancient
Llanystumdwy woods cast their spell upon Lloyd George. According to his diary entries he found in his youth that he could worship
better in the leafy tabernacles of the woods than he could in Capel
Ucha, and it was under their shade by the Dwyfor that he expressed a wish to be buried.

On the death of her husband Rebecca Llwyd had to deal with
the hard facts of life, and would have had no time to wander
through the woods. To her they had an important practical use as
the source of firewood. Had she been a woman of less courage
when she was left alone by the death of her husband with three
children to rear, she might well have felt that there was no option
for her but to throw herself on the charity of the parish. The 1841
census return shows how she responded to her predicament. It
records that there were then five occupants of the Highgate cottage: Rebecca Lloyd (aged forty); Elizabeth Lloyd (aged twelve);
Richard Lloyd (aged six) and Robert Morris (aged twenty—
journeyman cordwainer) and Richard Morris (aged eighteen—also
a journeyman cordwainer). Eleanor the eldest girl had been born in
1825 and was sixteen; when the 1841 census was taken, she had
left home and taken work as a maid on one of the farms in the
neighbourhood. Elizabeth, who was later to marry William George,
the Pembrokeshire schoolmaster, was twelve; and Richard, who
was to become the well-known Uncle Lloyd, was only six. Robert
and Richard Morris would have served their apprenticeship as
'journeymen cordwainers' and Rebecca had decided to employ
them in order to carry on the shoemaking business. It would
appear that a drover, David Rowland, was living next door, and he
must have been a good customer. (The trade of the drovers continued in Llanystumdwy and the surrounding district until 1867,

when it was killed in one fell swoop by the extension of the Cambrian Railway through Criccieth to Pwllheli.)

In his Welsh book *Richard Lloyd*, published in 1934, my father William George records what he had heard in the family about his grandmother Rebecca, who died in 1868 when William was three and David five. My father had a very early and rather terrifying memory of being doused vigorously by her over the head in a tub of water on the kitchen floor. David had a childhood memory of accompanying her when she was doing her round of calls on farmhouses in the district. In exchange for her bills, she sometimes received money and on other occasions she was paid in kind—in the form of butter or eggs. Richard used to tell the children what a wonderful and practical grandmother they had had, describing how she used to travel to Pwllheli to buy the leather and other necessaries to carry on the shoemaking business. She was a mistress who rose early in the morning to set her two journeymen to work, and, after putting the children to bed, she worked late at night by the light of her candle to make out her accounts on small scraps of paper—accounts which she delivered personally by walking from farm to farm and cottage to cottage along the atrocious roads. My father relates a story he had heard from his mother concerning Robert Morris. Without Robert's loyalty, it seems, the business might well have failed and he did not like being interrupted in his work. One summer's day a village gossip overstayed his welcome at the small workshop's open window. Robert Morris got up, explaining to the passer-by that he must close the window—'otherwise I'll lose what you never had, a good name'!

By the time the 1851 census was taken, Elizabeth had left home and was in domestic service in the Pwllheli district. The only occupants of Highgate cottage were Rebecca, described as head of the family and a 'Shoemistress' employing two men; Richard, a son, aged sixteen and David Lloyd (Jones), a grandson aged four. David Lloyd Jones was the eldest son of the daughter Eleanor, who had married William Jones, a Criccieth farmer. As often happened with large families in those days grandparents would 'adopt' one of the children to help out, and Rebecca had clearly decided to help Eleanor and perhaps repay her for turning out at such an early age, following her father's premature death. David is later referred to in letters William George wrote to Richard Lloyd and he was apparently a lad whose health gave cause for some concern. He died at a relatively early age and was buried in the same chapel churchyard as Dafydd Llwyd, after whom he had been named.

Rebecca had survived the Hungry Forties and her bereavement with rare ability; but for her there would have been no home and shoemaking business at Llanystumdwy, a home to which Elizabeth brought her husband William George, to whom she was married at Pwllheli on 16 November 1859.

The 1851 census recorded the relative strength of the various religious denominations in North and South Wales. There were only three Scotch Baptist places of worship throughout Wales and these were all in North Wales, the Criccieth chapel at Penymaes being one. Their total membership was 176. This contrasts with 478 Welsh Calvinistic Methodist chapels at that time in North Wales alone with a total membership of 105,146. Lloyd George was born into a family which, for at least two generations before his birth in 1863, had been conscious of being members of a very small minority indeed, a family of Scotch Baptists who spoke and acted in accordance with their convictions, regardless of the opinion of their neighbours.

The 1851 census also revealed that more than 75 per cent of the Welsh were nonconformists, and the statistics show that the great majority of the members regularly attended religious services on Sunday. For the Lloyd family this meant a walk of two miles each way between Llanystumdwy and Criccieth. Nonconformists generally gradually woke up to the significance of the 1851 census, particularly in relation to the oppression wielded by the established Church in exacting tithes for its support from the nonconformists. In the earlier years nonconformists had seen the Church of Rome as its main enemy, but in the latter part of the nineteenth century this enmity and distrust were directed towards the established Church, the Church of England in Wales; the parsons, the squires and their agents were then seen as the oppressors of the peasant farmers and quarrymen. The great religious revival which swept through Wales in 1859 brought many more within the nonconformist fold and gave an added impetus not only to religious fervour but also to the political awareness which followed in the wake of the religious revival. Once men secure the right to freedom in religious matters, sooner or later they will also demand the same freedom in the political and economic sphere. This is what happened in Wales in the second half of the nineteenth century, the period during which Lloyd George and other Radicals of the same generation were born and grew up. Lloyd George was, above all else, a realist, and it is important to remember that nonconformity during this period almost ran to seed in that far more chapels were built and proliferated across the land than were needed. Lloyd George was aware of this, and of excessive sectarianism, and it accounts for a great deal of the antipathy he showed in later years towards the faith in which he was bred.

The 1850s and 1860s were years of rapid development and industrialization throughout the whole of Britain, and there was a mass movement of population, particularly from Mid and North Wales into the industrial valleys of South Wales. Compared with the beginning of the nineteenth century, the population of Wales had doubled by the mid 1850s and the rapid progress of industrialization in South Wales was almost wholly responsible for this growth. In emigrating, as it were, from Pembrokeshire to the quiet of Llanystumdwy, William George was moving against the tide. When he came to live at Highgate, whilst earning his living as a schoolmaster at Pwllheli, six miles away, he was joining a family whose dependence on shoemaking as a means of livelihood was inevitably threatened by the output of the factories. Rebecca Llwyd must have lived long enough to have seen the demand for locally made boots dwindling, and she must have been pleased to see her daughter marry a schoolmaster, a profession which was just coming into its own. The Puritan faith of the Lloyds had given them an overriding belief in the importance of working hard and of self-help and individual responsibility before God and man for all our activities. William George came of a family of South Wales Baptists and he too took life and its responsibilities very seriously. Rebecca Llwyd, strong character as she was, would never have accepted William George into the household unless he had met with her whole-hearted approval.

CHAPTER THREE

WILLIAM GEORGE, SCHOOLMASTER

William George was the eldest surviving son of a Pembrokeshire farmer, David George of Trecoed, Jordanstown, a man of comfortable circumstances who was reputed to own another farm in the district. He had married a governess, Mary Charles. They had eight children—five daughters and three sons, one of whom died in infancy leaving William as the eldest and heir-at-law. David George died when William was about six. One would have assumed that subject to the widow Mary's right of dower, William would have succeeded to the farms on his mother's death—if not sooner, on his attaining his majority. Both my father and my uncle were aware that their father had somehow or other lost his inheritance. Their belief was that he was such an unwordly character that he had allowed the Statute of Limitations to run against him, and I remember my father telling me that, at their mother's request, on the advice of Mr. Goffey, a Liverpool solicitor, the boys had ransacked the cottage at Highgate for some acknowledgement or receipt or any other document which might have shown that their father had received during his lifetime some rent or profits from the farms or one of them. These farms include land which is now part of the Pembroke National Park, and I believe that Strumble Head Lighthouse is built on one of them.

Contrary to the natural expectations of the family of widowed mother and sisters, William took no interest in farming. After leaving school he was apprenticed to a Dr. Miller of Haverfordwest at the age of seventeen. It was the custom at that time for youths to work in a druggist's store before entering medical school to sit examinations. But William did not meet with Dr. Miller's approval because of his habit of burning the midnight oil to read books, thus making him less lively than he should have been in performing his chores in the store. He left Dr. Miller to become apprenticed to a draper in a village five or six miles away. As he was of delicate health, his mother bought him a pony so that he could ride to and from his work. However, this way of life did not suit him as he was too tired to study when he got home.

Haverfordwest is the capital of the 'little England beyond Wales', as south Pembrokeshire is called. And indeed William George's diary entries for the two months he kept them in June and July 1839 could well have been written in any English county town. They are revealing only of his own temperament and the honesty with which he records his utter sense of frustration:

Mon. 2nd June 1839 To-day began a very eventful week. The morning was spent between attending to my duties at the store and preparing myself for the theatrical performance to-morrow evening. Spent an hour alone after dinner, rehearsing my part. From then until six I was again occupied in preparing my dress etc. After tea attended the rehearsal which lasted till ten o'clock; did not get on very well with my part. I have not enough bustle and energy for it!

Tues. This morning again I was occupied preparing principally for the performance in the evening. Spent some time rehearsing my part; found that it did not at all suit me, and I was very low-spirited in consequence. After dinner I spent some time in the Store, went to the theatre to rehearse my part and I got through rather better than on the previous evening. Still I greatly fear a failure. Took some stimulants in the evening, hoping that I should get on better, but I overstept the mark and I did much worse than at either of the rehearsals.

Wed. Got up this morning at a late hour and with a severe headache. Felt deeply mortified at my failure the previous evening, for I cannot conceal the fact from myself any more than from those who witnessed it that it was a failure. I derive some consolation from the fact that some of the qualities of the Captain are those which it is no misfortune I do not possess. In the evening I attended the fireworks on the bowling green with my friend Mr. Brett.

Thurs. The whole of this day was spent in the usual monotonous routine of the business, until the evening when I went to the Harmonic Society's concert.

[The entries for Friday and Saturday are similar references to the business.]

Sun. The greater part of the morning I spent arranging my books, after which I got dressed and took a short walk before dinner. After dinner I spent some time at my a/c's. That done, I went for a long walk which I enjoyed very much, the weather being delightfully fine, —still I am not happy. I want enthusiasm, energy and *uniformity*. . . . Here ends the history of the first week of my Journal. It contains nothing but paltry commonplaces, but I hope that in a little time I shall improve.

The journal, in fact, from this point on becomes increasingly

37

disjointed, before the entries for 1839 peter out altogether within a few weeks. He is studying French, German and algebra. One evening in the gardens, after a lady had 'been playing the musical glasses very beautifully', he becomes involved in an incident, in which a Miss H. is insulted and this made him 'unhappy for the rest of the evening'. The following day he records he felt much concerned about her, and 'I have a great desire to write her or her grandmother a letter of advice anonymously.'

This incident appears to have triggered off a series of miserable days, and he records returning to his lodgings at 8 in the morning. 'Had not been to bed all night. Slept till 11.'

Fri. Rather late getting up, hardly got over the *spree* yet. Very sorry that this should have occurred and that I should have taken part in it all. . . . I have some thoughts of going to New Zealand.

Mon. Still very miserable. . . . Have done very little today, trying to get on with my algebra. . . . This illness makes me more unresolved than ever. If I don't do something, I don't deserve to live.

Wed. This morning I spent in translating, and made little progress. My radical defect is a want of unity and continuity of purpose. This is partly constitutional and partly due to my not having any being to whom I am strongly attached, in whom my affections are centred instead of wandering about.

The next stage in his career was to move to London—I presume in 1841—to become a student in the Battersea Teachers' Training Institute under a Dr. Kay. When he left after a year's training he gave a farewell address. His gratitude to Dr. Kay and the Institute is akin to that of a man who had just been rescued from drowning:

My friend Bragg has said that parting is a painful thing, and it is in this case, especially for those who have lived happily together for any length of time. In such a case no one can know how painful a thing it is until he has experienced it himself. I hope that I have contracted more than one friendship during my stay at Battersea, which will only terminate with life itself, nay not even then but that when we have quitted the present stage of existence, they will be renewed under happier auspices, and with greater strength and purity.

I have made these few general remarks concerning myself, and as I am but a poor, unpractised hand at public speaking, I would willingly end here if I could do so with propriety; but I feel it would be unpardonable of me to miss this opportunity to mention Dr. Kay, to whom I am so deeply indebted.

When I applied to Dr. Kay for admission to this Institute, I confess

38

that I had but a faint hope of success. I was an utter stranger to him, and I must add that my means were very limited. I made the application as an experiment—a last desperate experiment—to obtain what I had so long desired: for I had long wished to become a teacher and I felt that this wish had in great measure been responsible for destroying my usefulness in other pursuits. I had formed a thousand schemes to attain my object but all had failed, and I had almost given up in despair, when I read of this Institution. I then determined to make another attempt, thinking that if I failed, it would be only more disappointment added to the many I had already experienced.

I shall always regard the year I have spent in Battersea as the most important in my life, and this Institution as the means by which I was brought from a *miserable* useless life to one which I trust will be a happy one and not altogether destitute of usefulness to others.

The following year an open letter to 'The Welsh People' was published by Hugh Owen in London and was destined to have a decisive effect on the life of the young William George, in common with other young men of his generation who were seeking for some advancement in the educational opportunities open to them.

Hugh Owen was born in Anglesey but later moved to London. He became a legal executive with the Commission administering the Poor Law, and took a keen interest in the lot of the youth of Wales. In his open letter he urged the people of Wales to establish a British School in every district according to the system of the British and Foreign School Society, and he spelt out in considerable detail the steps to be taken to achieve this end. As a result of this letter, there was for some years considerable activity throughout Wales in the foundation of such schools. The letter was primarily directed to the nonconformists, particularly in South Wales for they were firmly entrenched at that time in their sectarian tradition that education was the exclusive preserve of their chapels, and they were not prepared to accept for their children any form of schooling supported by either the Anglican Church or State grant. Hugh Owen probably did as much as any Welshman in the last century to break down this kind of prejudice. He was a practical visionary, and took a leading part in establishing both the Teachers' Training College at Bangor in North Wales and the University College of Wales at Aberystwyth. A statue commemorates him at Caernarfon within a few yards of the statue commemorating David Lloyd George. If the two statues could exchange thoughts, Hugh Owen might well claim that but for his 1843 letter and the practical steps he took to implement his educational ideals, William George would never have become a school-

39

master in Wales, nor would he have met and married Elizabeth Lloyd and become the father of their son David Lloyd George; no letter, no David Lloyd George, no statue!

A few extracts from Hugh Owen's letter will explain its relevance to the situation in which the educationally starved young William George found himself in 1843:

Government Aid: Every man ought to know that the Government con- tributes about thirty thousand pounds annually towards the erection of schools, and that Dissenters enjoy full liberty to obtain part of this sum for the erection of British Schools. . . . I anticipate that the grant the Government can make will be nearly sufficient, in a country like Wales, where labour and building materials are so cheap, and especially where so much help will be given free of cost in the haulage of building materials, to build the school.

Teachers: It would never be worth entailing the cost and trouble of erecting the schools, unless care be taken to secure for them efficient teachers. . . . It is a task which no one ought to undertake without special training. There is in London a school for the instruction of teachers in the method of the British Schools, viz. the Normal School of the British and Foreign School Society. Eligible young men from Wales can obtain admission to this school. They would have to remain there for some months in order to make them efficient in their calling.

The response to Hugh Owen's letter was immediate, parti- cularly in North Wales: by 1852 there were ninety British Schools in North Wales and by the time the 1870 Education Act was passed there were 300 British Schools in Wales and the number of pupils were about 35,000.

I can find no reference to Hugh Owen's letter in any of William George's notes and letters. It is quite possible that he did not read it at the time it was published, but the British School at Pwllheli to which he was appointed in the 1850s owed its existence to Hugh Owen's letter and initiative. But before that stage in his career William George taught in various schools in England. After his year at the Battersea Institute he notes that he came 'to Ealing Grove School on Monday evening January 31st 1842' which must have been his first appointment.

That summer 'with the sole object of cultivating [his] own powers of expression', he recorded some of the thoughts, 'upper- most in [his] mind', in a notebook. When I consider that my grandfather did not live long enough to see his children outgrow their babyhood, and that he died nearly fifty years before I was born, these reflections of his have for me a timeless and poignant quality. I record them verbatim as they appear in his notebook. In

40

some ways, they might well have been written by a young, frustrated and lonely schoolmaster in Ealing today.

In proceeding with these exercises I do not intend to follow any
particular plan, but to write down anything and everything that occurs
to me at the time. I think it probable that considerable benefit will
result from this practice, for, by this means I shall see what is in me,
and have the privilege of being laughed at by myself only, without
exposing my nonsense to be laughed at by others. This is a principle
by no means to be despised, and one which, if it had been properly
appreciated by many of far greater talent than myself, would have
saved them from many a pang. There is another advantage which I
think likely to follow from this practice, namely that whatever nonsense I may utter, *there it will remain to stare me in the face.* (Friday
evening—W.G.)

Monday 6th June 1842 On Saturday I went to London with a view
to seeing Dr. Elliotson, but was disappointed. I was very sorry about
this, as I am getting to feel rather anxious about myself. I brought up
two or three specks of blood just before I went to London. They were
caused by playing with the boys. I went into the City accompanied by
John G. He has picked up a good many ideas about human life,
morals and literature. . . . I called at Rendall's, where I learnt to my
regret that Jas. Rendall's wife has not turned out very well. She is, I
am told, very fickle and spiteful, even towards her own child. Truly
the selection of a wife is a serious affair. How often may that poor
fellow have to repent his precipitancy! The more I think on the
subject of matrimony the more important does it appear to me. Three
or four years ago I would not have required a week to come to a
decision; but now, a year would hardly suffice. As a man advances in
years he becomes more cautious; he then hesitates before taking any
important step. If a youth of 18 or 20 falls in love, he would marry
without a moment's hesitation, but the man of 25 or 30 stops and
considers long and seriously before making such an important change
in his condition. He does not look on matrimony simply as a legal
means of gratifying his own passion, but he looks upon it as a very
important change in his condition, and one which is intimately connected with his future happiness or misery. We went together to a
Coffee House, where I read a rambling rhapsody in *The Atheneum* in a
review of *The Book of the Poets.* When we left the Coffee House, we
returned towards Exeter Hall. On our way we stopped several times at
old book-stalls. We proceeded to a shop in King Street, Covent
Garden, where a volume of Shakespeare, including his poems, was to
be had. I then procured a very pretty volume containing all the plays
and poems, for the sum of four shillings. Bye and bye I nearly suffered

a humiliating exposure, whilst conversing a few days before about purchasing a copy. Goodall told me that he had lately bought a copy and described the edition. I had seen some of them a few days before, and this combined with a little vanity, or rather the shame of acknowledging that I had no copy of Shakespeare, induced me to give him to understand that I also had lately bought a copy of the very same edition. There is no use in mincing the matter, especially to myself, for if I did not tell a direct and actual falsehood, I certainly conveyed a false impression to his mind, in that I deceived him. Now this is a very pitiful and disgraceful affair,—to be led in this way by a little vanity, and moral cowardice to say that which, if not an actual lie, was, at all events equivalent to it and equally culpable. I believe that by far the greater number of falsehoods are told from the same cause, i.e. the want of moral courage. A thing is often said in carelessness and then adhered to from cowardice or shame. Thus a person often tells a lie against his will; he makes a *lapsus linguae*, and does not find out his error until he has, in his opinion, gone too far. His pride will not allow him to acknowledge the error; he is therefore obliged to exercise his ingenuity to make his statement look as near the truth as possible. Now I am certain that I am as anxious to be honest and truthful as any person can be, still I frequently detect myself guilty of some little prevarication, equivocation or the like, which although they do not amount to actual falsehoods, they certainly hover very nearly upon the confines of untruth. All this is very lamentable.

I find that I really must write oftener. I must *record something*—have something to show myself for the time that is past—so that I can say that I lived and did something at a particular time past. In looking back upon my past life, I find it is all of such a dreary character.

12th June 1842 I am at present in anything but a happy state of mind,—in fact, I am rather low-spirited. This I attribute partially to my indifferent health, but principally to the want of congenial society. I have also become possessed of late by a strong desire to be married. This renders me discontented with my present situation,—my mind is unsettled, and constantly wandering off to this favourite subject. And yet I cannot make up my mind to it. The more I think of matrimony the more I hesitate and dread it. My affections are not sufficiently engaged. I do not love anyone with sufficient violence to be unable to think on the subject—*perhaps* more is the pity. I add this because I think it is a great blessing for anyone to be really and truly in love. I am convinced however that I shall remain unsettled until I have effected this dread change in my condition. I begin to feel the want of a *home*—to be surrounded by those to whom I feel that I am an object of interest. In short I want to be *loved*. That is an exquisite

42

pleasure, second only to the pleasure of loving. . . . I know, I feel that I have a capacity for love,—even now my long pent-up affections are struggling to find vent. I have become quite fond of that boy G. Speed, and would do anything in my power that would be likely to benefit him. I am almost ashamed to confess it to myself, but there was actually a secret pleasure mixed with the pain I felt at hearing of his father's death. I immediately found relief in the thought that it would now be very probably in *my* power to befriend him! There was a luxury in that thought. But to return,—Can I marry one for whom I have no affection? Or one whom I do love but has no corresponding affection for me? The obvious answer is,—such a thing would be not only unwise but criminal, for in either case it would mean almost certain misery to one of the parties if not to both. . . . There ought to be such a confidence and sympathy between husband and wife as would induce them to reveal the inmost secrets of the soul to each other,—a confidence that would induce the husband to make his wife the depositary of all his little schemes of ambition (and what man is without these?) with the assurance of receiving a smile of approbation and approval.

Husband and wife necessarily spend so much time in each other's society, that if there should be no sympathy between them the inevitable consequence will be that they become disgusted with each other. Truly love is blind, and it is well that it is so. For what happiness could we enjoy if the imperfections of those we love were constantly forced upon our notice and making us uncomfortable. I have been thinking whether a high degree of domestic felicity is not calculated to promote too much contentment—to render one too satisfied with his lot—No, I see the fallacy of this at once,—it cannot have such an effect, not necessarily, at all events, as many illustrations to the contrary testify. All the same domestic happiness is not absolutely indispensable, as many instances show. The fact is—When a strong mind is resolved upon the accomplishment of any object, it will not be deterred even by so great a calamity as domestic unhappiness.

An ambition to be a good writer is truly a glorious one,—it is an ambition the object of which is to bequeath to posterity a legacy of 'thoughts that breathe and words that burn'.

19th June I am still very unsettled in my mind as to my future plans and prospects. I cannot somehow make up my mind to be a schoolmaster for *life*. My present position does not altogether satisfy me. I want to occupy *higher ground* sometime or other. I want to increase the stock of my attainments but hardly know how to set about it.

3rd July 1842 This morning I came to a resolution of writing a little every day, if possible. I may occasionally be able to record my own feelings, though but imperfectly at first. I shall acquire skill by degrees. And as these feelings are constantly changing, it will be an interesting exercise to watch these changes attentively. I shall thus become more familiar with myself—with those feelings which most habitually predominate in my mind and influence my conduct. This knowledge will be valuable as a guide to the knowledge of others' characters.

31st July 1842 I am far from being in a contented frame of mind just now. The principal cause of this dissatisfaction is my indifferent success in the school. I feel the want of more extensive and exact information than I possess at present, as well as more energy and activity in communicating it. The latter defect I attribute in a great measure to my indifferent health,—to the necessity of setting a constant watch over myself, and of measuring all my actions and movements. But if I should recover my health perfectly, that objection will then be removed, and in that case I must resolutely aim at a higher standard— to do more or nothing at all. . . . As a preliminary to this it is important that I should decide upon the subjects to be studied and form some plan for pursuing them.

In the first place, I think that I am tolerably up in *Grammar*, so that I may feel easy about that.—Geography also, I am sufficiently advanced to keep ahead with very slight preparations.

The journal breaks off here and is not resumed until 1854. So far as my records go, William George did not fulfil his 'resolution of writing a little every day'.

From his pencilled notes I was able to discover that he left Ealing Grove School in December 1842, and that he came to 'Newbald on Saturday evening April 1st, 1843; left for holiday 15 August '43. Returned again Sept. 5th 1843. Left finally March 25 1844.' He then lists forty-seven of his possessions which he left at this school, including Johnson's *Lives*, a volume of Shakespeare's plays, Brougham's letter on national education, and a life of Napoleon. He gives no explanation for this apparently extraordinary abandonment of his books and other personal belongings. He tended to list details for I also found a scrap of paper inside the cover of one of his notebooks giving a minute account of the journeys he made between the time he left Ealing in January 1843 and his arrival at Newbald in April the same year, together with careful details of every fare. He went to London, Tunbridge Wells, Bishop's Stortford, Cambridge and had two months' holiday in Pembrokeshire and altogether his fares came to £8 7s 3d!

Lady Byron appears to have had some part in running the

Newbald school: he has a diary entry for 13 June 1843, 'Cash from Lady Byron £10'. During the year he spent here he also kept a meticulous account of every item of expenditure, even noting that tooth powder and hair oil cost him 10½d, haircut 3d, tobacco 6d, communion 6d and 'the Englishwoman 1s'. When he left at the end of March he paid 6d for 'ale and biscuits on the road' and 1s 1d for 'dinner in London'. Still, at the end of the year he had sufficient in the kitty to buy himself a watch costing £8. In May 1844, home once more in Pembrokeshire, he pays a Haverfordwest tailor £2 17s 0d for a suit and buys a bonnet for his mother costing 7s.

By the late summer of 1844 William George had returned to London and had bought quite a number of books to replenish the stock he had left at Newbald. He also bought himself a greatcoat for the winter costing £3. The entries peter out that September. The next entry is 'Expense of Journey from Wales July 15 & 16, 1846'.

	£	s	d
Dinner		1	8
Biscuits, drink, book		3	2
Steamer & freight	1	0	6
Brandy		3	0
	£1	8	4

William George's movements from one district to another are so frequent and unpredictable that his recorded notes afford only occasional clues to his whereabouts. What makes him so elusive is his almost complete detachment from his home at Trecoed. He refers indirectly to this himself in a letter he wrote in 1858 to a Welsh Baptist Minister in Pembrokeshire. By then he was teaching in the British School at Pwllheli.

I wished to say a few words to you in Welsh—but I am sorry that I cannot do so, although Welsh is my mother tongue—and I knew very little English until I was nine years of age—but I have used English almost ever since. The English language has done with me what the English people have done with our country—taken possession of the richest and largest part of it. No sooner do I use two or three Welsh words than their bolder English brethren thrust forward and the poor timid Taffies shrink back to hide themselves and I cannot, in spite of the utmost effort, find them again in time.

I do know that at Christmas in 1852 a copy of *Webster's Dic-*

45

tionary was presented to him by 'the teachers and conductors of the Children's Service of Hope Street Church Sunday Schools as a token of respect and esteem on the occasion of his leaving'. This is inscribed on the presentation copy of the dictionary. I have always understood that William George had been in Liverpool teaching for six years before he left in 1852. The Hope Street Sunday Schools were administered by the Unitarians whose leader in Lancashire was James Martineau, the Unitarian divine and professor of mental and moral philosophy at Manchester New College. For many years William George had been a reader of periodicals, such as the *London Literary Gazette* and the *National Review*. Meeting and becoming friendly with James Martineau and his sister Harriet who were both contributors to these periodicals must have been a stimulating experience and at some point James Martineau presented him with a framed and signed portrait of himself.

Of more practical importance to his future family than his association with the Martineaus was the friendship he formed with Thomas Goffey, a Liverpool solicitor. He may well have consulted Goffey concerning any entitlement he might have had to his deceased father's property in Pembrokeshire. From the copy Inland Revenue Account filed by Goffey after William George's death in 1864, it appears that he had invested £640 in Liverpool building societies. His notes show that he was paid a salary of £100 for 1849 anyway and it would have been impossible for him to have saved as much as £640 out of such earnings after paying his expenses, so it seems that Goffey must have retrieved some of his lost Pembrokeshire inheritance for him. His total estate when he died amounted to £768 so, presumably on Goffey's advice, he must have invested all he had in the building societies. The interest from this modest investment was his widow's sole source of income in bringing up her three young children. Otherwise the family was completely dependent on Uncle Lloyd's small shoe-making and repairing business. Goffey was also the clerk to the Governors or Trustees of the Hope Street Schools and signed the letter inviting guests to attend the meeting at which the presentation to William George was made. He was given not only *Webster's Dictionary* but also an oak bookcase containing all the volumes of the *Penny Encyclopaedia*.

His six years in Liverpool were probably the most settled in his life and his circumstances were easy enough in 1850 for him to lend '£40 to Trecoed', that is, to his mother and stepfather. Considering that this was nearly half his annual salary, it was a generous loan, made apparently without any security or strings attached to

46

it. At the beginning of January 1852 he had £40 in hand and by the end of the year over £50. There is no indication why he left Liverpool. His health, never robust, had probably deteriorated and he may have left on medical advice. Although Liverpool was the first city or town in the country to appoint a medical officer of health, Dr. W. H. Duncan in 1847, it must still have been an unhealthy place in the 1850s. Public Health legislation was only in its infancy. From its first appearance in Sunderland in 1831 until well into the 1860s, cholera was frequently epidemic; in 1848–9 it killed at least 130,000 people. An extract from the Report of the General Board of Health in 1849, gives an indication of the insanitary conditions prevalent in cities and towns;

Householders of all classes should be warned that their first means of safety lies in the removal of dung-heaps and solid and liquid filth of every description from beneath or about their houses and premises.

William George must have been aware of the need to provide better sanitation because one of the items he purchased was a water closet! Presumably his landlady also benefited from this purchase, both before and after he left Liverpool in January 1853.

There is no record how he spent his time in 1853. I infer that he must have returned to Pembrokeshire and to the family home whilst he recuperated and searched around for another teaching appointment. An undated scrap of paper between the leaves of his notebook may well have been written at this period of uncertainty as to his next job:

Have to-day felt a strong reaction against an inclination for farming—because I haven't sufficient means I should be obliged to submit to a very humble life and many privations—because I should find the life a very dull one—and because farming unfavourable to intellectual pursuits.

A Stationer's shop at H'West—publish an almanac (Welsh)—send it to fairs and markets—also a monthly mag. price 2s—'The Cambrian Chronicle' of facts and opinions. . . . OR Bookseller's shop in Fishguard. Write down all that occurs to me about further course. . . . Think of Liverpool—Liberty and independence of such a life.

He did not, in fact, buy or rent a printer's or bookseller's shop, with the 'liberty and independence' he fancied such a life might bring in its wake. What he did was to open a school in Haverfordwest at the beginning of April 1854. His draft advertisement read:

ENGLISH SCHOOL
for
Scientific and Commercial Education
—HAVERFORDWEST—
conducted by Mr. William George
Trained and Certificated Teacher.

* * *

I call that Education which embraces the culture of the whole man, with all his faculties—subjecting his senses, his understanding and his passions to reason, to conscience and to the evangelical laws of the Christian revelation. Dr. Fellenberg.
Mr. George having received a regular training at a Normal College, has enjoyed superior advantages of studying the most improved modern systems of Education. [Then follows a comprehensive list of all the subjects which are necessary to a sound and complete English education.]

Great attention will be paid to the study of the English language, a knowledge of which is now indispensable to the successful pursuit of every business and profession in this country. Much useful general knowledge will be imparted by conversational lectures, suited to the capacities of the pupils, and illustrated by diagrams and experiments.
Terms: One guinea per quarter.

There is a Welsh couplet:

Disgwyl pethau gwych i ddyfod,
Yn groes i hynny maent yn dod.
(Expecting great things to come,
They are contrary when they arrive).

Which sums up my grandfather's experience on opening the school as recorded in his notebook:

5th April 1854 Arrived at Haverfordwest on Monday to open a school—Much annoyed at having missed my way as to the preliminaries—would have been much safer and avoided the appearance of failure if I had remained in the country until I had a sufficient number to begin with.

Another mistake was to fix a uniform charge of a guinea a quarter. Better to divide the school into three sections—to take all who offer—charge 20s a qr. for the 1st. 15s for the 2nd & 10s for the 3rd. This will perhaps produce an average of 15s.

In 1847 government-appointed commissioners had reported on the state of education in Wales. The report was known in Wales as

'Brad y Llyfrau Gleision' (The Betrayal of the Blue Books).* It revealed, amongst other things, that of the teachers then conducting schools in Wales only about 10 per cent were trained. On the face of it a teacher with William George's training and education should have made a success of his school and attracted more pupils than he could manage. His failure to conduct the school for more than two or three years must be attributed primarily to the educational system of the day, under which the school was dependent financially on local voluntary contributions. As practically everyone acknowledged, this was a wicked system which was not put right until the 1870 Education Act.

Again, William George's reference to having been trained in a 'Normal College' would have created prejudice against the school amongst the Anglican community, who saw in the British and independent schools a threat to their own church or national schools. William George was really getting the worst of both worlds: he was teaching outside the Establishment, typified by the Anglican Church, and also without the approval of the nonconformists in South Wales who held strong views against any form of education under government patronage. One of their leaders, the Reverend David Rees, declared:

I do not hesitate to say that any system of general education under the patronage of the Government is as certain to prove a curse to the country in the future as the existence of the Church of England is a curse to the country at the present day.

William George's notes in the early summer of this year show that in spite of his responsibilities in running the school he must have had sufficient time to renew his previous practice of writing down his thoughts on paper. His ambition to be a writer was revived but he felt that he was far from realizing that ambition: 'Very desirable to write much more frequently remarks which are suggested in private reading. Should not be too particular what to write about—it is constant *practice* that gives facility, no matter what the subject.' He refers to Oliver Cromwell as an Orator:

A deeply political, practical and precise intention animated all his words, pierced through their confusion, pervaded all their windings; and he impelled his auditors with resistless force towards the object which he wished to attain, by exciting in their minds, at every step, the impression which it was his object to produce.

---

* H.M.S.O. published the report in volumes encased in blue. It caused an outcry throughout Wales.

Anyone who heard Lloyd George speaking in the House of Commons or addressing a packed audience in the Caernarfon Pavilion would acknowledge that he had cast his own style of oratory in the same mould. He would have read through his father's notebook when he was a youth in Llanystumdwy. It is impossible to say how much influence this particular quotation may have had upon him, but I am sure the effect of the sum total of his father's reflections and recorded quotations was considerable. His father's insistence on '*always* having writing materials at hand when you are reading' was certainly a precept which he obeyed.

William George's comment in his notebook on an observation by Lord Bolingbroke shows that he regarded life as a serious, although not necessarily a solemn matter. Lord Bolingbroke:

I have observed that in comedies the best actor plays the droll, while some scrub rogue is made the fine gentleman or hero. Thus it is in the farce of life. Wise men spend their time in mirth; it's only fools who are serious.

William George comments:

This observation would be true *if* life were a comedy or farce; but it is not. Life is a very serious business to most men. To be serious is frequently a sign of true wisdom.

The following observation shows that he deplored the use of sectarian religion as a political weapon:

It was said by a former King of Prussia that, as we are intellectually blind, the Deity sent us religion to guide us on our way; but instead of using it as heaven intended, we began to labour each other with it.

One of the most cryptic references in his notebook at this period is the following:

'Perhaps, however, it's all for the best—my present false position so uncomfortable that I can hesitate no longer—shall speedily be *forced into a decision*. **(On that point.)**'

The emphasis on these words are his. There is no written record in our family papers to explain what important decision faced him when he started the private school in Haverfordwest, but I was told by my father that he married a widow many years older than himself in Haverfordwest. She was in some way connected with the premises where he established his school. Her name was Mrs. Brown and she was consumptive. My father told me that she had fallen deeply in love with William George. His motives in marrying her are not known, but this extract from his notebook suggests that

50

he had found himself in a position where his marriage was in some way connected with the school. The extract comes immediately below the extract, already quoted, announcing his arrival at Haverfordwest to open a school.

There are three undated and apparently unrelated references to the subject of marriage in his notebook, clearly written about the same period. The first:

'Everywhere but in novels', says a recent writer, 'the marriage of convenience has proved an excellent institution; while what are generally called love-matches have been, are and ever will be prolific of misery. They spring from passion and terminate in early satiety. The romance disappears—the sentiment subsides—the woman remains!'

The next:

Qualifications of a Wife. 'If you marry', said an uncle, 'let it be a woman who has judgement enough to superintend the work of her house, taste enough to dress herself—pride enough to wash herself before breakfast—and sense enough to hold her tongue when she has nothing to say.'

The third:

'Beauty', says Lord Kaines, 'is a dangerous property,—tending to corrupt the mind of the wife, though it soon loses its importance over the husband. A figure agreeable and engaging, which inspires affection without the ebriety of love, is a much safer choice. The graces lose not their influence like beauty. At the end of thirty years, a virtuous woman who makes an agreeable companion charms her husband more than at first. The comparison of love to fire holds good in one respect, that the fiercer it burns the sooner it is extinguished.'

These quotations and thoughts suggest that the marriage was not a love-match on his side, but there is nothing to support the oral tradition in the family that he did not expect Mrs. Brown to live more than a few years and that he had married her out of pity. The probability is that he married her when he was thirty-two and when she had lost the lustre and beauty of her first youth. She probably was, like himself, in poor health, and this may have been a bond between them. In fact, she died within two or, at most, three years after the marriage; and in January 1857 William George writes from St. John's, Wakefield, to the Revd. W. Roberts concerning another school appointment.* William Roberts was a

---

* The original of this letter is with the Revd. Roberts's papers deposited in the National Library of Wales at Aberystwyth.

Baptist Minister and the representative of the British and Foreign School Society in South Wales. His church was at Blaenau in Monmouthshire and between 1854 and 1865 he was busily establishing British Schools in South Wales. The last paragraph in William George's letter to William Roberts reveals that he had been offered the post of second master at the Blaenau school (spelt Blaina in the letter):

St. John's, Wakefield.
21st Jan. 1857

Rev. Sir,

I duly received yours of the 24th ult° but I thought it better to defer my reply until after my return hither, as I might then be able to say when I should be likely to be at liberty. The time is not fixed, however; and I do not intend to say anything more on the subject to the Committee before I have another school in view. If I heard soon perhaps I might be released at Easter.

With respect to the salary, I should not be disposed to take much less than £60 a year. I understood that as much, and sometimes even more, is given to masters of lower schools (which I should prefer). I know that the master of the National School in the small town of Haverfordwest had £60 a year, a house and garden, with coal and candles. However, one of my chief considerations in desiring to move is my health; and a good school in a healthy locality would be a more important object than an extreme salary.

The situation of Second Master of the Blaina school would not meet my views.

I remain, Rev. Sir.,
Your ob^t Servant,
W^m. George

Rev. W. Roberts.

I do not know how long he stayed in Wakefield or why he was there. This letter is the only evidence I have of his movements between closing down the Haverfordwest school, presumably after the death of his first wife in 1855-6, and his appointment as master of the newly opened British School at Pwllheli.

Notes and extracts from letters he wrote at this period show that his search for health was why he kept moving from place to place. An undated note records:

Happiness is a requisite for health. It is happy therefore that this at least is within our reach. We may be confined to close and narrow homes, shut up in cities and cut off from the sweet face of nature and the pure breath of heaven; to regulate our diet may not be in our

52

power; exhausted by sedentary toil, exercise may seem almost for-bidden to us, and baths a luxury hardly to be thought of, but happiness may be ours; for it lies in doing good.

In April 1858 I think he must still have been in Wakefield. The following is the first of a few extracts, copied by my grandmother, of letters he wrote at this time:

April 1858

My dear Mother,
I send my portrait by this post, and if you admire it, you can hang it up by my other portrait which you have at Trecoed. . . . To me the face appears to wear an expression of great earnestness, as if I were occupied by some business of pressing importance. . . . Well, I am trying to joke a little and perhaps it is best for me to do so, though I assure you I am far from well.

Yesterday was a beautiful day. I went for a walk but though I did not walk very far, I felt quite tired on the way back and the friends who were with me had to give me some help.

I must look for a small school in the country as soon as my time is up here.

I understand that following the receipt of this letter his mother and stepfather went to see him at Wakefield. They must have helped in getting him to leave for some time after August 1858 he moved to Pwllheli and wrote to his mother from that town, describing a meeting with a visiting preacher:

A Rev. Mr. Williams of Liverpool was here last Sunday—collecting for the mission of the Welsh in London, helped by Mrs. Jones and her son—who are considered amongst the first people in Pwllheli. They have taken a good deal of notice of me. They've invited me to sit in their pew every Sunday and they invited me to supper last Sunday. There I met Mr. Williams—I reminded him that we had met before at the house of Mr. Nicholas Fishguard. As soon as he knew I came from that neighbourhood, he asked me about many persons I knew there.—He asked did I know Mrs. Williams of Trecoed—*pobl dda, caredig iawn* [good, kind people]—When I told him: 'Mrs. Williams is my mother,' he jumped out of his chair.

When he left he gave me a warm blessing. My dear mother, I need not tell you how pleased I was to hear him say that you were one of the best women in Pembrokeshire before that good company.

My situation here is still much the same. The school gets on very slowly, but I am beginning to get acquainted with some of the people and I find them very kind. Last Thursday and Friday the Methodist Association was held here. I am told that there is usually a very large

53

gathering—on occasion from 10 to 15 thousand. I heard the most eloquent preacher—'The Great Gun'—as some of the people called him. He related a conversation he had with a very intelligent brother in South Wales on the introduction of the railway into his neighbourhood. This brother related several changes it had caused and amongst others that it had equalized prices there with those in the capital—And so, he said, the advent of the cross had equalled the prices of heaven with those of earth. Before *His* coming the most precious spiritual things were either unknown or regarded as worthless among men. He followed his text and in his style of oratory there were occasional passages of fervid eloquence. However, he never seemed to struggle with the weight of great thoughts. All his gold seemed to lie in glittering grains on the surface; one watched in vain for an occasional monster nugget dug up fresh from the depths below—There was real gold however. Often as I have heard of the love of Christ as manifested in His suffering, I have seldom heard it described with greater effect.

This was the last letter he wrote his mother of which there is a record. She died in 1860, and the inscription on her grave in the churchyard at Jordanston reads:

Mary George, subsequently Williams, of Trecoed: died 1860 aged 78. She was a faithful member of the Baptist church at Llangloffan for upwards of 45 years, was a genuine Christian and obtained a good report of all men and of the Truth itself.

In a letter he wrote to a cousin, Captain Williams of Fishguard, William George referred to the health of his sister Mary:

I have heard of you frequently from Anne and from Trecoed. I believe I have not written a single letter from here to Pembrokeshire without enquiring about Mary's health. I was glad to have a better account of her lately. I hope she will be restored to health, but her constitution like mine is not made to last long. I suppose neither of us can expect a long life. But whose life is long? Some people live a few years longer than others, but after all, what is the longest life compared to eternity? A mere drop in the great ocean—my grandfather was 92 when he died—I have often been touched with the words: 'All the days of Methuselah were nine hundred and sixty nine years; and he died.'

When we think how short a time we have to live in this world, it is a wonder we should allow it to engross all our thoughts and affections as we do. We cling to it as if it were our greatest good and shrink from the thought of leaving it. No doubt this strong love of life has been planted in us for a wise end. This world seems to be intended as a sort of apprenticeship to teach us how to live in another world. How little do most of us learn of our heavenly calling—But this love of life is only for this world. We must overcome the fear of death; unless we do so, we cannot meet death calmly. Yet many religious people cannot bear to think of death.

The last extract I have from letters he wrote when he was at Pwllheli before his marriage to Elizabeth Lloyd, is from a letter he wrote to a schoolmaster. I have no idea who the schoolmaster was, but the letter is interesting on account of the light it sheds on William George's attitude to the Bible and religious belief:

I hardly know what to advise as to the course you should pursue in the school—Your opinion of the value of the Bible as a religious text-book appears to be lower than mine now is. I was at one time prejudiced against it by the writings of the Socialists and controversies etc, with which I have now little sympathy indeed. I have lately been in the habit of writing down a little of the Book itself, and am getting back into the old opinion that as a source of instruction on the spiritual nature and destiny of man, there is no book in the world to be compared to it.

I have very little doubt that this will be your opinion too, when you have gone through your allotted share of the discipline of sorrow and humiliation.

William George's reference to the socialists in this letter indicates that he had been influenced by Bentham and the first socialist, Robert Owen. Owen had been born in Newtown, Mid Wales in 1771. In 1799 he married the daughter of a wealthy mill-owner in New Lanark on the banks of the Clyde. His friend Bentham assisted him financially to acquire a controlling interest in the mill business, which he then ran on a completely new, profit-sharing principle in partnership with the workers. Owen taught that labour is the source of wealth and that men would be unable to live peaceably together until they realized how misguided they had been by the religious ideas to which they were bound by tradition. Owen became known in nineteenth-century Wales as 'Mr. Owen, the Atheist'. Consequently, although his co-operative enterprise at New Lanark became internationally known, he exercised little influence during his lifetime inside Wales itself. William George was as a Welshman exceptional in having fallen under the influence of Bentham and Owen, but after considerable soul searching and introspection he came to believe that the Christian religion, properly practised, enshrined the socialist ideals pioneered by Owen and others.

CHAPTER FOUR

FIRST-BORN SON

The British School at Troed-yr-Allt, Pwllheli, had advertised in 1857 for 'a master required to teach the Classics, French, Mathematics and Navigation; he must either have, or be prepared to take a Government certificate of competency'. I assume that the committee failed to find a master who miraculously combined all these qualifications for William George was not appointed until sometime in 1858. My grandmother Elizabeth Lloyd, known to her contemporaries as Betsy Lloyd, was at the time in service with a Miss Evans who lived at Y Castell (The Castle) in Pwllheli, next door to Troed-yr-Allt school. She had many years previously left her mother's home at Highgate as a young girl to enter domestic service in the Pwllheli district. The Baptist chapel at Pwllheli, in the immediate vicinity of the school, was without a resident minister at this period, and it was this which brought William and Elizabeth together. Amongst William George's papers there are notes of several addresses on religious topics, and he probably helped out by speaking at the chapel services from time to time. Neither Elizabeth nor he, however, were enrolled as church members at Pwllheli, and they were married at St. Peter's, the parish church, Pwllheli, on 16 November 1859.

Following their marriage they made their home with Elizabeth's family at Highgate. When the 1861 census was taken they were still living there. He was described as a 'British Schoolmaster'. The other occupants were Rebecca Lloyd, 'shoemakeress', described as head of the family, her son Richard Lloyd, and her grandson, David Lloyd Jones, described as a 'scholar'. Life in the small three-up and two-down cottage must have been exceedingly cramped. Water had to be fetched daily and carried in buckets from the village pump; the earth closet, at the far end of the garden, was an unpleasant necessity, and as the railway was not extended to South Caernarfonshire until 1867, the village highway running immediately in front of the house would still have been covered from time to time with the dirt of animals driven by the drovers towards the nearest rail-head. Before moving to Pwllheli and Llanystumdwy William George had already encountered life in the raw, but his life in Liverpool had been more sophisticated both

56

materially and socially and he probably felt intellectually starved and physically inconvenienced by the realities of life with his in-laws at Highgate.

One of the few surviving records of William George's life at Llanystumdwy during 1859–61 is a fragment of a letter his friend and solicitor, Thomas Goffey wrote to him. The fragment is un-dated, but a reference in it to English involvement with Garibaldi's revolt indicates it was written in the autumn of 1860. What has survived of the letter reveals not only the close friendship between William George and Thomas Goffey but also refers to the birth of the Georges' first-born at Llanystumdwy, a fact which has not been mentioned in any of the Lloyd George biographies. I have checked this reference with the entries on the fly-leaf of the Lloyds' family Bible, and this states that a girl—their first-born—died and was buried at Capel Ucha, Criccieth. The child is un-named, which indicates that she could not have survived for more than a few weeks.

The death of this child may have been one of the factors which unsettled the Georges and prompted them to leave Llanystumdwy during 1861 for Newchurch in Lancashire, where Mary Ellen, their second child, was born on 8 November 1861. They had lived at Highgate for less than two years, and probably concluded that Elizabeth's second confinement might well follow the fate of the first, unless they moved to a larger house. Moreover William George's knowledge of Welsh was very limited, as he freely ad-mitted, and by moving to Newchurch, he would be nearer to the circle of friends he had made in Liverpool.

They probably travelled, with their belongings, by stage-coach from Pwllheli to Caernarfon and then by steamer from Caernarfon to Liverpool. It was quite an anxious journey and an ordeal for Elizabeth George, leaving her native county for the first time. She must also have wondered what effect the journey might have on her second pregnancy. If something went wrong on this occasion, it might really be the end of the road for her, on top of the chronic asthma she suffered from.

When they moved they took their nephew, David Lloyd Jones, with them for Richard Lloyd and Rebecca were hopeful that he would qualify as a teacher with William George's assistance. David's exercise book for 1860 shows that William George was already giving him detailed help with his work, but William George himself did not feel confident that his nephew would make it. For one thing he did not have a sufficiently robust constitution to fight his way to the top in the battle of life and also William George had noticed that he had been spoilt at Highgate by his grandmother. Had he been a selfish man he would have refused to take David with him to Newchurch. But one can also see something of what he was from his farewell address to the children and staff at Troed-yr-Allt school. (Moreover to have refused would have meant that he was not prepared to practise what he preached.)

To do good, to be useful and beneficial to others, to be of a kind and obliging disposition, tender and compassionate, to feel for the wants and miseries of others, so as to be ready to relieve them,—this certainly is the happiest and noblest temper in the world. Narrowminded and selfish persons think their own happiness the greater because they have it alone to themselves.

What can we do? We can give nothing to God, because he stands in need of nothing. But though God himself has no need of our services, our fellow who is made in the image of God may have need of them; and it is by our goodness to men that we can best show our gratitude to God. To be a benefactor is to be like God as 'tis possible for men to be. And the true advantage of greatness and wealth and power does not consist in this, that it sets men above others, but that it gives them the power to do more good than others. Men often call them their *betters* who are higher or richer than themselves; but only those are really our *betters* who do more good than us.

And now, children, if you believe this saying of our Lord that 'It is more blessed to give than to receive,' try to act accordingly. Do not excuse yourselves by saying you see very few follow this rule of conduct. That is unfortunately too true. If we are to judge of men's opinion by their practice, I am afraid it will appear that few believe this to be the way to happiness.

The Lord Jesus was not like the scribes and Pharisees of whom he said, 'They say and do not'; this was his constant practice, the great work and business of his life. He who pronounced it the most blessed thing to be good, spent his whole life in this work, and 'went about doing good', giving herein an example that we might follow his steps. He would not so much as have any fixed abode and habitation, that he might be at liberty 'to go about doing good'. He received nothing but injuries and affronts, base and treacherous usage from an ungrateful world. The whole business of his life was to do good, and to suffer evil for so doing. . . .

William had shown this careful composition to Richard Lloyd before it was delivered. He had been greatly impressed and only regretted that William could not speak Welsh well enough to stay in Llanystumdwy and eventually help his co-pastor and himself in the unpaid ministry of the Baptist Church.

They moved to Newchurch in the spring or early summer of

1861, and William George's first letter to Richard from Newchurch is concerned almost wholly with David's state of health. The following is an extract:

> I took him today to the Doctor to see if he would give him something else to settle his stomach. He examined him again carefully—more carefully than he did the time before, and he told me after David had gone out that his constitution is rather delicate; that he will require great care to be taken of him while he is growing or else he will go into consumption, but that he cannot find there is any disease in him yet.

The letter concludes with William thanking Richard for sending them the Welsh weekly newspaper, published then as now in Caernarfon, *Yr Herald Gymraeg*, which, he said, 'interests us very much'.

His next letter to Richard Lloyd, written in August 1861, shows that he was awaiting a talk 'soon with Mr. Davies, the Inspector of Schools, about removing to another school'. Richard was anxious that he should return to a Welsh school, but William was non-committal in response to this suggestion. On 10 June 1862 he was still at Newchurch and wrote to Richard, mainly concerning David's impending return to Llanystumdwy for a month's holiday. He said it was time 'David girded on his armour to begin life's battle in down-right earnest'. Concern for David's welfare is the main thread running through their correspondence. In this June 1862 letter William George gave no hint that he was very unhappy at Newchurch and searching almost in desperation for another teaching appointment. The only one he could find on offer was a temporary post to take charge of a school connected with a textile mill in Manchester. The headmaster was ill, and until he recovered sufficiently to take full charge of the school once more, William George was asked to run the school with the assistance of four pupil-teachers. In October he wrote to Richard from Manchester at considerable length explaining the removal from Newchurch. A few extracts from this letter reveal the deplorable state of elementary education in the 1850s and 1860s; the pay was exiguous, the working conditions a constant threat to the teacher's health and the methods of instruction in the three Rs were mechanical and soul-destroying. To an imaginative, widely read and thoughtful teacher like William George the constant deferment of any effective reform of the educational system was profoundly depressing. He wrote:

> You may be sure that we were both very glad to leave Newchurch.

The place itself we could do with very well—though cold and rather damp, it is healthy—the air is much purer there than at Manchester, and neither of us could hold out long without pure air. It was the Newchurch *school* and the people connected with it that did not suit me; and I need not say that I did not suit them. Nearly all the 'Directors' are rough working men who had not the means to act liberally even if disposed to do so,—and besides my temper is such that I would rather be the master of work people than their servant. . . .

I don't know anything more with respect to my position here, I don't even know what they are going to pay me . . . I don't remember whether I told you before that these schools are connected with large print works, perhaps the most celebrated of their kind in the Kingdom. It is at these works that 'Hoyle's Prints' are produced. Every draper tries to persuade his customers that the gown will wash well because it is one of Hoyle's Prints. . . . The present head of the firm, Mr. Arthur Neild, is 'my Committee'. I have heard them spoken of as very kind gentlemen and liberal to those who please them; but if anyone displeases them once, he may adopt the motto over the gates of 'Dante's Hell'—'Let all who enter here abandon hope.' I hope for their own sakes that they are not quite as unforgiving as they are said to be. . . .

I have had my hands quite full with this large school (we have about 170 with 4 pupil-teachers). I might remain here myself till next spring or early in the summer. . . .

[After referring to the necessity of David henceforth making his own way and that he could not arrange for him to follow him immediately from Newchurch to Manchester]—I went to London when I was younger than David, and I well remember how wretched I felt for the first few weeks—I got better then. All who go out to the world to fight their own way must go through this hardening process, and the sooner the better. The griefs of early life are often very bitter but they are almost always of very short duration in comparison with those of after years.

In another long letter he wrote in November 1862 to his cousin Anne James of Fishguard, congratulating her on her engagement to master-mariner Captain Williams, also of Fishguard, William George wrote in a much lighter vein. He referred to Anne's description of her future husband in a letter to Elizabeth and himself:

Your Aunt *was* very curious to have some idea of his personal appearance. As for that one eye that is but a slight defect—especially as Capt. W. can make such good use of the remaining one. That he can still see very clearly, your Aunt needs no better proof than his choosing you in preference to any of the eager beauties which surrounded him

60

(you might almost take the words in their military meaning) at Fishguard. . . .

It would give me very great pleasure to be present on the happy occasion but it will depend upon the *time* whether I can or not. I think I can say now that I shall not be able to come so far from home during the month of January and perhaps February,—before or after those months, if alive and well, nothing should prevent my coming. . . . I must leave off to nurse little Mary—the storm has been rising for the last few minutes and now it is *raging*.

The reason William George could not travel to his cousin's wedding at Fishguard in January 1863 was that Elizabeth was expecting her third child in January. On 12 January William George wrote another long letter to Richard. Although Elizabeth's confinement was now imminent, he made no reference to it. As the letter was almost wholly concerned with matters of family interest, this was a curious omission, which can only be attributed to the extreme reticence in mentioning anything to do with generation or birth, characteristic of my grandfather in common with many other Victorians. He was extremely reticent also in referring to his own state of health, but there are one or two significant pointers in this letter that he felt far from well:

The Master of this school is better—he came in twice last week, and was in the school for about 1½hr. today. He says he is all right, but I think he is very far from 'all right' and shall be greatly surprised if ever he gets strong and well again. . . . There is very little doubt that he is consumptive, but he is cheerful and almost free from pain as consumptive people often are, and also so often blind to their own danger. Merciful blindness, when they are dying by inches, for months, perhaps years. I expect he will soon recover sufficiently to return to his duties for a *short* time. Then cometh the end. Poor fellow! I am very sorry for him. *I may go before him,* but it seems to me that his lease of life is almost certain soon to expire.

When he wrote this letter William George had decided to give up teaching and to take a small farm in south Pembrokeshire. This was to be his last effort to regain his health and to settle down with his young family. Richard had sent him the *Caernarfon Herald* so that he could have a look at farms which were going vacant in Caernarfonshire.

William replied: I suppose you meant to give me a chance of speculating in one of their small farms for sale. I have not sufficient confidence in my judgment to *buy*—I would rather rent one.

C

In a reference to his wife and their baby daughter Mary, he wrote, as if to underline the message of the family's *physical* frailty:

Little Mary still keeps the best of the family, it's wonderful. It is true her mother is very careful of her and that no doubt has much to do with her good health. I do not think she is naturally strong—how could she be? Can strength come out of weakness?

Nevertheless when, on 17 January 1863, Elizabeth gave birth to their first son—David Lloyd George—at 5 New York Place, Robert Street, Manchester, strength *did* come out of weakness. They called him 'David Lloyd', the same Christian names as their adopted nephew's. William George must have known by this time that David Lloyd Jones was consumptive and William was doing his best by letter to warn Richard Lloyd and the grandmother in Llanystumdwy that the high hopes they had entertained concerning the boy were not likely to be realized because of the lad's delicate state of health and in fact he died at the age of twenty on 2 September 1867 and was buried at Criccieth.

A few days after David Lloyd II's birth William wrote to Richard:

I am happy—very happy to say that Betsy and the young gentleman continue to get on very well. Betsy got up at about 5 this afternoon and she is still up, for which I am scolding her. I tell her she is over-doing it the first time.

Little Mary is not thrown on one side although a son and *heir* (!!) has arrived. The dear little thing is getting more interesting every day. She is certainly a very sharp child. . . . She has taken wonderfully to little David. She calls him *boy, boy* and she gives us much amusement by mocking him when we ask her—how does boy cry.

The woman who is here to wait upon Betsy is very kind to Polly [this was a family nickname for Mary Ellen the baby daughter]—almost the only thing that is in her favour. She is not a good hand at preparing a bit to eat—she used to work in a factory.

I am glad to say that I am better. My throat has not gathered as I feared. I have been poulticing it till it is nearly raw outside, but that is better than being inside.

> Love to all, Yours Ever truly,
> Wm George.

In an undated letter written two or three weeks later, William George replied at some length to Richard Lloyd's letter, in which he had related the details of a division in the ranks of the Pwllheli Methodists. William George was as much of an anti-Methodist as Richard Lloyd himself, judging by the following comment:

62

We both greatly enjoyed the account of the state of things at Pen-mount. The Seceders have been outwitted very cleverly. 'When rogues fall out honest men may get their own', and the disgraceful proceedings of them Penmount Methodists will, I hope, open the eyes of many to see the real character and natural tendency of their system and thus promote the interests of true religion.

There is no reference to the 'son and heir' in this letter, but in the concluding paragraph he says:

We are all pretty well. Betsy was rather weak the first fortnight but I think she is gaining strength now. She drinks bitter ale and finds it does her good. We cannot get good milk and she was tired of drinking tea all the time, especially after some extraordinary tea the nurse gave her. She thinks it must have been some cold tea boiled in a saucepan. That dose was a *sickener*.

I don't know exactly when we shall be leaving here or where we shall be going next. . . . As soon as I know for certain what our next move will be I shall let you know. If I take a school it will be only as a temporary convenience—I shall give up teaching and get into the country as soon as I can.

William George and his family moved from Manchester to take the tenancy of 'Bullford' a smallholding in Pembrokeshire in the spring of 1863. The annual rent was £30 and the smallholding comprised a farmhouse, outbuildings and thirty acres of arable and pasture land. It was well situated within a mile of the G.W.R. station at Johnstone. Significantly, William George had chosen to settle in the southern, English-speaking part of Pembrokeshire. The family home of Trecoed was in the northern, Welsh-speaking district of Pembrokeshire. Perhaps in settling in a different part of the county he was also showing his determination to plough his own furrow right to the end.

Amongst the family papers in my possession there is only one letter written by William George whilst he was at Bullford. This is a letter to Richard Lloyd dated 23 August 1863 and is mainly about Thomas Goffey's efforts to get David Lloyd Jones appointed to the Hope St. School on trial. He adds that the governors are very anxious to secure David's services, but are worried about his health. One of the reasons they were anxious to have him was: 'The second master, an Irishman, has no command over the boys, and no wonder, for the master found him the other day dancing in the school for the amusement of the scholars in school hours!'

William George says not a word in this letter about his family nor does he refer to his own health. We are left in the dark as to whether or not he had had reason to regret the removal to Bullford and the abandonment of his teaching career. The concluding paragraph of this letter is an appeal to stay-at-home Richard to visit him and his young family in south Pembrokeshire.

You said something a week or two ago that you had often thought of coming to see us. My dear Brother I hope I need not say how delighted I should be to see you, but I had given up asking because I had no hope of succeeding. It would do you much good to go from home for two or three months, for I fear you are wearing yourself out. If I could say anything to induce you to come here, be sure I would soon say the word. Won't you give me a hint how to set about the formidable task of persuading you?

In spite of the pressing invitations Richard received, he did not make the journey to Bullford during his brother-in-law's lifetime. What was clearly meant to be the beginning of a new lease of life and health for William was, in fact, the beginning of the end. At the end of May 1864, after being out in the fields during the hay-harvest, he caught a severe chill. His wife had seen him ill many times before; he was lucky if a month went by without some minor illness assailing him. If they had sent for a doctor every time he was ill, they would have spent what little capital he had invested in the Liverpool building societies. This time it was different; after taking to his bed and running a high temperature he started to have difficulty in breathing. On 2 June Dr. J. D. Brown of Haverfordwest was sent for. He pronounced William George to be gravely ill and told Elizabeth he could not hold out much hope—the chill had turned into pneumonia. William George died on the 7th; Elizabeth was shattered. She managed to send a telegram to her brother, containing two words only—'*Tyrd Richard*' (Come Richard).

William George's stepfather, farmer Benjamin Williams of the old home at Trecoed in north Pembrokeshire, arranged for him to be buried with Elizabeth's consent in Trewrdan cemetery, where his father David George, who had also died in his forties, was buried. Trewrdan cemetery, near Trecoed, is about twenty miles to the north of Bullford and Elizabeth probably stayed with the two children at Bullford. Dr. Brown had advised her to take extreme care; he could seldom have been called to a more defenceless family. Probably Elizabeth did not know then that two or three weeks before her husband died she had conceived the fourth and last of her children. This child, born posthumously on 23 February 1865, was my father William George, who was destined to live to within one month of his hundred and second birthday.

A draft of the first four pages of a letter Elizabeth George sent Thomas Goffey, instructing him to take out the Letters of Administration of her husband's estate, for he died intestate, has survived amongst the family papers. It sheds considerable light on the hard facts of the situation:

BULLFORD

(Undated)

My Dear Mr. Goffey,

I am greatly obliged by your kind letter received the 18th inst. Indeed I cannot tell you what a source of consolation it has been to me in my deep affliction—Well I may believe that my dear husband was your 'dearest friend' and that he was highly esteemed by all his friends there, for such he always considered you and his respect for all his friends in Liverpool was very much. It is a comfort to me to think how much he was beloved by all his numerous friends. Oh! What a dear husband I have lost.

As Mr. George's opinion of the Haverfordwest Attorneys was not very favourable, and that you kindly offered me your service, it is with many thanks I am sending you the information for taking out the administration. Mr. Williams, Trecoed [stepfather] came on Friday and he took the valuation of the stock, furniture etc. He said he used to do it. It is now they are sowing the turnips. Mr. Williams says that the crops, if not gathered in, need not be included under such occasions. . . . It is only two cows we have got at present and only the kitchen and one bedroom we have furnished.

Mr. Williams (my husband's stepfather) repeated his promise of the house to me and my brother on Friday—That I shall have the rent until the little children will become of age. I gave him a broad hint to have it in the children's name. I don't know what he will do and I must be careful in that as you well know he is very eccentric.

I cannot tell you now when I leave the South—We are trying to find a person to take the place that will pay me something for the lease—and to take the crop under valuation. . . . Some months ago my dear husband thought he was going to lose me—When I recovered he said—I was walking about without knowing what to do. If that would be the case I was determined to leave the place at once—I couldn't think to stop on a day here but it was me that was to stay and how hard it is upon me to be here after him—The little children's health is pretty well, and myself as well as it could be expected. It cannot be very good for some time. . . .

Soon after writing this letter it appears that Williams and

Goffey took the situation in hand. On 15 August a sale was held at the holding; the furniture realized £34 and the farming stock £57. In October the lease and crops were sold to an incoming tenant for a total of £64. As I have mentioned my grandfather had £640 invested in various Liverpool building societies and the tenant of a small Pembrokeshire cottage, which he had inherited, paid £90 arrears of rent held back during William George's lifetime. After deducting the expenses, the net estate amounted to £768, and Letters of Administration for an estate under £1,000 in value were issued in favour of the 'lawful widow and relict', Elizabeth George. Early in October 1864 after assigning the lease to Mr. John, the new tenant, Elizabeth and Richard, with the two small children, made the long trek northward to Llanystumdwy. The furniture had been sold, but William George's extensive library had not been included. The decision by Elizabeth and Richard to preserve these books and carry them northwards, at whatever cost and inconvenience to themselves, was probably the most important of all the decisions they took—certainly, the most far-reaching in its consequences. A letter, written by my uncle, David Lloyd George, to my father over forty years later describes a visit he had just then made to Bullford:

BUNKERS HILL
MILFORD HAVEN

September 18th 1905
My dear W.

Drove to Bullford this morning. Dr. Griffith met us at Tiers' Cross, close to the little Congregational Chapel, which I was told my father often attended. He was very friendly with the Minister—a Mr. Thomas.

The farmer who bought the lease from poor mother met us—a Mr. John. Very nice fellow. He brought with him the Assignment of the Lease which he gave me. Very nice little place, with a touch of real style about it. Most untidily kept. Mr. John told me that its present appearance gave no idea of what it looked like. The trees on the drive all cut down. I saw the gate Mary and I carried stones to—not the old gate. That has been taken down and part of it put up elsewhere. Dick took photographs. It all rather saddened me.

Cei'r hanes gan Dick [Thou will get the story from Dick].

Fyth, [ever]
D.

The incident to which my uncle refers in this letter occurred on the day of the sale of the furniture. It must have been a traumatic experience for the children, Mary and David, to see the pur-

66

chasers carrying away their mother's furniture in bits and pieces. Their attempt by placing small stones across the path to obstruct their passage was one of the very few incidents concerning her life in Pembrokeshire their widowed mother was prepared to discuss in later years with her children; my father told me they realized that their mother found it too painful to answer their questions about their father and her life in Pembrokeshire, but she always told them what a good and kind man he was.

In retrospect, the sadness of frustrated ambition and unfulfilled hopes pervades the life of William George. The numerous books and tracts he had purchased on education and educational reform suggest he should really have been a university lecturer; the many quotations in his notebooks show that history was the subject which appealed to him most. The notes of addresses he had prepared and read to children reveal a genuine concern to convince them of the importance of living a life of service to others. He was distressed by the narrow sectarianism which bedevilled every effort in his lifetime to achieve a radical reform of the educational system. During 1857–8 the school at Troed-yr-allt, Pwllheli, to which he was appointed, had been the centre of a local sectarian row, and the *Caernarvon and Denbigh Herald* of the period carried references to the dispute in its correspondence columns. On 27 June 1857, an Inspector of Schools wrote begging the 'townspeople to forget their differences and unite in forming a vigorous school for the town, where a good secular education shall be supplemented by religious instruction, based upon the only word of Life'. There is no evidence that he took any part in this or in any other dispute. The unhappy atmosphere at the school engendered by this dispute, and the sectarianism, which he deplored, probably contributed to his decision to leave Pwllheli and Llanystumdwy so soon after his marriage.

His own attitude towards the place of religion in education is summed up by the following quotation, which he noted with approval, extracted from Matthew Arnold's correspondence:

I allow as fully as you can do that the University [of London] should include Christians of every denomination without the slightest distinction.

He was doomed to spend his teaching days in the 1840s and 1850s, when teachers were discouraged to teach anything much beyond the three Rs and when the authorities were afraid that the effect of passing the long overdue measures of educational reform would cause the labouring masses to become discontented with their lot and insubordinate. He was a man born at least half a century before his time, and his hope of seeing a more enlightened system of education must have been finally dashed when the Department of Education adopted the offensive 'Payment by Results' system of remunerating teachers—the desired results being almost wholly limited to the pupils' progress in assimilating the three Rs. This was in 1861, following the publication of the report of the Newcastle Commission. This report even put in a good word for child labour! What he must have felt to be excruciatingly humiliating was the necessity to keep his learning to himself, and he was probably laughed at when he tried to impart to pitifully illiterate children something of his own love of history and poetry.

The response of the pupils and the Government Inspectors to efforts by William George to raise the level and quality of his instruction did not serve to dissipate the downright drudgery and monotony of his daily round of teaching. I tend to think it was his hand which folded over two pages in one of his books, *The Classbook of English Poetry*. He was very fond of poetry and this must have been a book to which he turned frequently in the rustic solitude of Bullford. The first marked quotation is from *As You Like It*—'The Exiled Duke's Philosophy'.

> *Sweet are the uses of adversity,*
> *Which, like the toad, ugly and venomous,*
> *Wears yet a precious jewel in its head;*
> *And this our life, exempt from public haunt,*
> *Finds tongues in trees, books in running brooks,*
> *Sermons in stones, and good in everything.*

The second marked quotation from this anthology is from Goldsmith's *Retaliation* (proposed epitaph for Edmund Burke). As he reflected on his own march through life, he may well have thought that this quotation, and particularly the last line could also serve as an epitaph for himself:

> *Who, too deep for his hearers, still went on refining,*
> *And thought of convincing, while they thought of dining,*
> *Though equal to all things, for all things unfit:*
> *Too nice for a statesman, too proud for a wit;*
> *For a patriot too cool; for a drudge disobedient;*
> *And too fond of the right to pursue the expedient.*

CHAPTER FIVE

BOYHOOD

Within a few days of the sale of William George's furniture and farm stock, Richard and Elizabeth with the two young children, Mary Ellen and David Lloyd, started on the long trek northwards, by rail as far as Caernarfon via Chester, and thence to Llanystumdwy by carriage from Caernarfon for the last eighteen miles of the journey. William George's library of books packed in teachests formed the largest item amongst the luggage with which they were burdened. It would have been so easy to have left these awkward boxes behind, and the responsibility of looking after two young children with Elizabeth by now nearly five months pregnant would have been ample justification for their decision. As it was, they packed not only Shakespeare's plays but also history books, such as Green's *History of England*; Burnet's *History of the Reformation* (six volumes); eight volumes of *The Pictorial History of England*, published in 1847, by Charles Knight; a complete set of the *Penny Encyclopaedia*; a well-bound presentation volume of *Webster's Dictionary*; *The Journals* of George Fox; many English language and other textbooks; and several books on education, such as *The Philosophy of Education* and the Commissioners' Reports on the state of education in Wales published on behalf of H.M. Stationery Office in 1848; Arnold's *Life and Correspondence* (two volumes); *The Schoolmaster—Essays on Practical Education* (two volumes); some volumes of The European Library series, such as *History of The English Revolution* (1640) by Guizot; Hallam's *Constitutional History* (two volumes); several anthologies of English poetry and the Bible, given to him before he left Trecoed in 1834. It is evident that William George's interest in books was far wider than that of the average British schoolmaster of his generation. He had built up his library by devoting a substantial proportion of his small income towards it and the transport of his library from one home to another during his frequent moves was an additional drain on his slender financial resources.

Had this library not been brought from Bullford to Llanystumdwy I am sure the history of our family would have been entirely different. The library stayed at the Llanystumdwy cottage home until 1880 when it was moved to Criccieth and the bulk of it is now in my possession. These books were always readily available to the George children for careful study. There is no better testimony of their educational and civilizing influence on the children than a notebook which was the joint property of the two brothers. William started writing at one end of this notebook and David at the other, and both continued to do so until they met in the middle.

Both were pursuing the same method of absorbing the contents of the books they read by writing a chapter-by-chapter précis. In his half of the notebook William wrote a précis of some of Macaulay's essays, and of the *Theory of Moral Sentiments* by Adam Smith; David wrote a chapter-by-chapter précis of Green's *History of England*, at times in writing so small that a magnifying glass is needed by a person of average eyesight to decipher it. Paper was in short supply, and throughout their lives both brothers, like their Uncle Lloyd, had acquired a habit of using every available scrap of paper and making notes, sometimes, on the oddest pieces of paper, such as the inside of used envelopes; the joint notebook had started life as the account book of a friendly shopkeeper. When they started keeping detailed diaries, both brothers used the back of discarded official documents such as electoral lists.

David's précis extended to forty-one quarto pages and he recorded at the end: 'Finis—3rd July 1879. 873 pages.' He was then sixteen. The last chapter in the précis is on Ireland, and when he wrote: 'Irish constitution a counterpart of the English', he could not then have dreamt that he was destined to play a decisive and controversial role in the framing of a new Irish constitution which kept some semblance of harmony in Ireland for nearly half a century.

When the carriage bringing the shattered family back to Llanystumdwy stopped outside Highgate in 1864, and the 'Head of the house, Shoemistress Rebecca Lloyd' welcomed the bereaved family into her small home, she must have been shocked by the amount of space William George's book-filled boxes demanded. Her knowledge of books was probably limited to the family Bible.

Rebecca was then in her sixties; she was a practical woman, widowed early like her daughter, but she was made of sterner stuff than Elizabeth. It was due to her efforts that the shoemaker's business, established in the 1820s by Dafydd Llwyd, was still in 1864 sufficiently thriving to employ two men in addition to her son Richard. He had taken after his father Dafydd Llwyd and in Rebecca's opinion spent too much of his time on things which were not of this world. That explains why she had continued to employ two men, even after Richard Lloyd had grown up and could, had he been a dedicated, full-time shoemaker, presumably have taken the place of one of them. Elizabeth's tragic home-coming would have been even more tragic had Rebecca Llwyd retired, as so many now do on reaching sixty, and allowed the business to be run by her son after he had come of age. As it was she was in a position to keep the business going during Richard's four months' absence and thereafter to succour her daughter and the young children during their early years. She remained in complete charge of Highgate and the shoemaker's business until her death on 19 June 1868 twenty-nine years after the death of her husband.

There is very little documentary evidence available of what life was like for the Lloyd George family in Llanystumdwy between 1864 and 1879; the brothers' notebook shows how they turned to their father's library for instruction. The landlord of Highgate was David Jones—the owner of the village shop. In later years he became one of the first clients of the brothers' firm of Lloyd George & George, Solicitors. It is worth while recording that the Georges' landlord was this village shopkeeper of modest means, and that he in no way typified the landowner against whom David Lloyd George in years to come was destined to aim his slings and arrows. The rent of Highgate was only £7 a year and for that rent David Jones did not expect to do any repairs to the house, particularly internal repairs. His working formula was: 'The rent is mine, the house is yours.' My father, in the biography of Richard Lloyd he wrote in 1934, recalls that the kitchen oven in Highgate had become practically unworkable during his boyhood and that before she could bake the bread every week, his mother had to contrive somehow to cover up the holes in the oven by using brown paper and paste. Sometimes the brown paper went on fire before the loaves were fully baked, but more often than not the baking was concluded when the singed brown paper burst into flames, and she would exclaim as the loaves were extracted from the oven, that her 'widow's devices' had won the day. On these successful occasions the crusted loaves sounded like a drum when she rapped them. The treat for the children was to dip the crust of a well-baked loaf in buttermilk before eating it.

There were times after the death of Rebecca Llwyd when the defective oven and lack of ready cash were more than Elizabeth George could cope with, and when he was eleven years old, my father remembered seeing his mother reading a religious periodical which obviously gave her great comfort for her face was transfigured from an appearance of grief to joy after she laid the paper aside. Years later, my father was able to trace the article and its purport was that the orphan and the widow had a Father and a Judge to whom they could always turn. He was merciful towards the widow and orphan, but merciless towards their oppressor.

I have already mentioned that my father lived to within a month of his hundred and second birthday. After he had turned a hundred there were times when his immediate environment slipped away from his perception and he returned to Llanystumdwy to relive some of his childhood experiences. The two brothers had slept in a wainscot bed; a week or so before he died my father banged the wall of his bedroom with the stick he kept at hand to draw my wife's attention or mine. I was the first into his bedroom on this occasion. He was back in the wainscot bed and had woken with a start on realizing that his brother Dafydd was not alongside him. He thought I was Uncle Lloyd and asked me to light a candle, saying (in Welsh): 'Has Dafydd got up?' He was afraid he had over-slept, would be late for school and get a caning from David Evans, his Llanystumdwy schoolmaster.

Llanystumdwy school was established in July 1851. The foundation managers were the Bishop of Bangor, Sir Hugh Ellis-Nanney and Miss Catherine Priestley (both the latter then Llanystumdwy landowners). The Rector was also on the Board of Governors. The trust was declared to be: to suffer the school to be used for the education of poor children, always in union with and conducted upon the principles of the established Church. The Catechism was to be taught and no scholars were to absent themselves. As the great majority of the children attending the school were from nonconformist families, this requirement was the cause of some friction between the Church authorities and the non-conformists in the district. The nonconformists were proud of the great efforts made by their predecessors to win the right to worship in accordance with the tenets of their particular denomination, often at considerable risk to themselves. Indeed during the boyhood of my father and his brother there were several people still alive who remembered an incident when a shot was fired through one of the windows of the Calvinistic Methodist chapel at Bontfechan, about a mile from the village, during a religious service in 1832.

The school was opened every morning with a series of prayers from the *Book of Common Prayer*, and the day's work closed with a similar series of prayers. These were read in English, and English was the only language used as a medium of instruction. Each child brought a penny or two a week with him to school as a contribution towards the headmaster's salary. The remainder of his salary depended on the outcome of a report by one of the Government Inspectors—the 'Payment by Results' system. In preparation for this day of inspection the headmaster, who was an excellent disciplinarian and knew how to get the last ounce of work out of the children, really put the pressure on. When the great day arrived and the inspector walked into the large class-room where the children were assembled, all the children sprang to their feet, the boys bowing before him and the girls making a curtsy. 'Good morning, sir,' they chorused before they were permitted to sit again. This performance invariably won for David Evans, the headmaster, the first accolade in the inspector's report: 'The children were neatly dressed, clean and very well behaved.'

Another important annual event at the school was the Scripture Knowledge Examination. Scripture was the headmaster's favourite subject, and both David and William remembered the dramatic effect with which he used to relate Old Testament stories in preparation for the visiting inspector's viva voce examination. A particular favourite was the story of Abraham leading Isaac up the mountain to be sacrificed to God and the heartrending conversation between father and son as they walked together towards the altar. With his upraised cane Mr. Evans personified Abraham as he was about to kill Isaac, and at this moment one of the girls had been told to scream, representing the voice of the angel who intervened at God's behest to save Isaac's life. David Evans then drew the moral: 'Abraham's obedience to God was absolute, my children, and so must yours be.' Both brothers in their turn won a first prize for their answers at this annual examination. My father was given *Sunday Evenings at Northcourt*, and David a *Treasury of History and Biography for the Young*.

David Lloyd George entered the school when he was three and a half, in September 1866. He stayed until July 1878, and the school log-book records that he left 'to be articled an Attorney'. This was no vague declaration of intent, but an accomplished fact, for at the surprisingly early age of fourteen David had passed the preliminary examination of the Law Society, and this fact was also recorded by the headmaster in the school log-book. My father followed suit about two years later during his last year at the school.

This exceptional achievement by two elementary school children shows that David Evans's teaching went far beyond instruction in the three Rs. He taught them Latin, as he was well qualified to do, and in addition, having realized that they were both exceptional pupils, gave them individual tuition in arithmetic and algebra at a special table, close to his desk, which he reserved for two or three outstanding senior pupils each year. He must have discussed the prospectus for the preliminary examination with Uncle Lloyd and made it clear to him that the one subject he had no knowledge of was French; accordingly the boys taught themselves this subject using a French primer which William George had bought for

David Lloyd Jones (who had now died) and a French-English dictionary. My father told me that Uncle Lloyd used to keep them hard at work, and woe betide them if they played truant. Mr. Evans and Uncle Lloyd knew how to put a cane to good use on occasion but the really telling factor was their uncle's force of example for Richard Lloyd himself struggled alongside them to pick up the rudiments of the French language.

A schoolmate of David Lloyd George's, Thomas Jones, told John Hugh Edwards, M.P. what kind of boy David was at school and he in turn quoted this description in one of the earliest Lloyd George biographies, published in 1913. It is quite clear from this description that Thomas Jones felt it was time to introduce some realism into the legends which were beginning to grow around Lloyd George's name: 'He was known among his school mates as David Lloyd. . . . In his early years at school David Lloyd was not as quick as some of his classmates. I distinctly remember that Humphrey, The Mill, Bob Felin Bach [The Little Mill], now a tutor at Oxford, I believe, and David Owen, Braich-y-Saint, were quicker than he was in some respects, but undoubtedly David Lloyd surpassed them in general knowledge. He was always to the fore in geography and arithmetic. His weakest point was his penmanship, which his companions used to describe as 'crow's feet' (*traed brain*). In his early years he was not as devoted to outdoor games as is suggested in some quarters. On the contrary he was quite a bookworm. After tea he would remain in the house poring over his books and especially the Scriptures under the direction of his uncle, while the rest of us would be indulging in games. Herein lies the real secret of his intimate knowledge of the Scriptures and the ease with which he is able to weave biblical references into the texture of his speeches. . . . Most of the children would only carry one book to and from school, but he would always have a whole bundle under his arm. . . . His demeanour was always one of marked quiet.'

One of the most vivid memories I have of my father, was one autumn evening in 1966, two or three months before he died. He would often be silent for long periods, and on this occasion he found himself back in Highgate. He broke the silence:

'I was sorry for Mr. Evans this morning.'

'Mr. Evans?' I asked.

'The old school,' he said, adding rather impatiently: 'You remember him, of course.'

'What happened?'

'Well, Dafydd preventing us from saying the Catechism, of course, with the Trefan ladies, Ellis-Nanney and all the nobs there.

74

BOYHOOD

I would have been glad if the floor had given way under me in the silence. It was awful. Dafydd is a terrible boy sometimes.'

This was a reference to the best-known incident in the school life of the two brothers. The incident occurred about two years before David left school, on the occasion of the annual visit by the school governors and local gentry to hear how well the children could repeat the Creed and the Catechism. It was apparent to the headmaster by this time that David should be apprenticed as a pupil-teacher in the school. Every three or four years, according to the school log-book, a boy showed sufficient promise to be apprenticed as a pupil-teacher whilst he was still at school, and this opened up for him a career in the Church or as an Anglican teacher in school. It meant, of course, that the aspiring cleric or teacher must change his denomination and become a member of the Anglican Church, if his family were not already of that persuasion. When the headmaster, with the best intentions in the world for David's future, mentioned this possibility to Uncle Lloyd, the proposal met with a frigid, if not openly hostile, reception. His reply, which was perfectly true, that this was the only recognized way for a promising pupil to win promotion, did nothing to modify Uncle Lloyd's attitude. In David's presence this staunch and uncompromising Dissenter accused the church authorities of attempting to proselytize the nonconformist youth of the parish of Llanystumdwy by these methods.

Following this, David organized a conspiracy of silence amongst the pupils, the overwhelming majority of whom were nonconformists. On the day of the governors' visit they did not recite the creed and would not reply when the headmaster asked them for their reason. There was consternation amongst the visiting platform party, who turned on the headmaster as if he were responsible for this unheard-of demonstration. This was more than my father could bear; he had the highest respect for Mr. Evans, and in an outburst of sympathy for him broke the silence by repeating the opening words of the creed: 'I believe . . .' The rest of the children followed suit. They did not want to see the popular Mr. Evans put publicly to shame.

One or two of the biographies on Lloyd George relate that he gave my father a sound thrashing afterwards for breaking the conspiracy of silence. There is a note in my father's handwriting commenting on this embellishment of the story:

This is unjust both to the brothers and to the story. As a matter of fact, the protest had been carried far enough to be effective, and David was strategist enough even then to realize that victory pressed

75

beyond a certain point was apt to defeat its own purpose. He had moreover enough chivalry to recognize the courage and independence of spirit which his younger brother, acting according to his lights, showed in 'breaking the strike', as and when he did. Anyhow, it is satisfactory to learn that the Nonconformist children at this 'National' school were never again called upon to stand up in the same way for their own and their parents' faith.

The importance of this early incident was that it acted as a kind of catharsis and purged the school of its imposition of the Church of England Catechism and Creed on nonconformist children. It was Lloyd George's first bold and successful revolt against injustice. In its conduct and conception he revealed that the child is truly the father of the man. Here was a young realist who believed, at this early age, in taking effective and ruthless action to achieve a measure of religious freedom in a situation which he had experienced at first hand. I say 'ruthless' because he was not prepared to allow his gratitude to the headmaster for the special tuition he was receiving to stand in his way of acting in a manner that was bound to humiliate and ridicule David Evans in the presence of the school governors. The means he adopted could, he thought, be justified by the end result.

Quite apart from its wider implications, this incident also introduced a note of realism into discussions regarding David's future. Any lingering hope that David and William might enter one of the professions by becoming pupil-teachers was finally dispelled. Shortly before the incident, Mr. Edwards, the village rector, had approached the brothers in the expectation that they would consent to become members of the established Church. About thirty years later when he was President of the Board of Trade, Lloyd George wrote to his brother referring to a schoolmate who had attained high office in the Church of England having started life as a nonconformist:

My recollection is that he started by going to Church once on Sundays and then gradually slipped over altogether. That was the offer made to us, if you recollect?, by the old parson.

When this offer was reported at home my grandmother is reputed to have said that she would rather see her boys growing up to break stones on the roadside than to see them turn their backs on the little Baptist chapel at Penymaes.

In the Lloyd George story his headmaster emerges as a principal character without whose expertise and dedication as a teacher neither David nor William would have been able to pass the preliminary examination of the Law Society. A lesser man than

David Evans would have been deeply offended by the militant anti-Church views of the youth Lloyd George and his family, and thereafter taken umbrage by confining his tuition strictly within the limits which were at that time appropriate for the great majority of the pupils. He was not expected by his governors to walk the extra scholastic mile with any child, except on those rare occasions, once or twice every three or four years, when a boy showed sufficient promise to be a pupil-teacher within the established Church; that he should have done so in the prevailing sectarian climate of his generation within these two out-and-out nonconformists is to his everlasting credit as a teacher and broad-minded churchman.

When my father was reliving some of his childhood experiences, he frequently referred to the excellence of David Evans as a teacher; what struck me on these occasions, when past experience and recollection merged into one, was that the injustice of the religious system no longer rankled in my father's mind; but he always deplored the way the Welsh language had been banished from the curriculum of this and every other school.

In the early 1870s Hugh Ellis-Nanney, the local squire, was building a mansion on a select site to the north-west of Llanystumdwy village. Frequently on a winter's morning the brothers in their wainscot bed would awaken to the sound of the waggons, carrying building materials to the site from Criccieth station. My father could remember getting out of bed to look through the small cottage window at first light to see the heavily laden waggons, drawn by three and sometimes four horses, trundle noisily past Highgate.

I asked him what kind of people these local landlords were, in reality, during his boyhood:

We only used to see them from a distance or at the annual inspection at school, he said, but the Trefan ladies were a picture when they were driven through the village in their carriage by the cockaded coachman. They allowed us to roam their fields, without anyone ordering us off, provided we respected the birds and the livestock and didn't allow Bismarck to chase the sheep. We had also to give the birds every chance to rear their fledglings.

We did think that that palace Ellis-Nanney was building for himself and his family, the work going on year after year, was much too big for the needs of any one man, but, who would have thought then that in 1890 Dafydd was to keep Ellis-Nanney from entering Parliament by only 18 votes, after a recount?

Throughout their years at Llanystumdwy Elizabeth George

kept in touch with Thomas Goffey. The children were annually reminded of his importance, because he was the only person singled out by Richard Lloyd and Elizabeth George to receive a Llanystumdwy-bred turkey as a Christmas gift. The three children, as part of the Christmas preparations, had to help to pluck the bird and parcel it for despatch to Liverpool. I cannot tell whether or not Mr. Goffey ever suggested that the boys should take up the law as a career. All the indications are that he must have done so, and told Elizabeth and Richard that they could draw on the building society funds to pay the stamp duty and premiums payable on entering into articles of clerkship. This would be a good investment for the future. Goffey controlled these funds and forwarded the small income to Highgate regularly. To use more than half of the investment to pay the premium and stamp duty (£180) firstly on David's articles and then a similar sum on William's was a calculated gamble, but one which their knowledge of the world would have suggested as sound; as the old proverb has it: 'No lawyer dieth a beggar.'

Another link with the legal profession was Myrddin Fardd, a local antiquary and a mutual friend of both Richard Lloyd and Edward Breese, a Fellow of the Society of Antiquaries and a partner in the Porthmadog firm of Breese, Jones and Casson, family solicitors. The founder of his firm was his uncle, David Williams, who had been closely associated with W. A. Maddocks during the early years of the nineteenth century. Maddocks had died in 1828, greatly impoverished after spending his large inherited fortune on the planning and development of the town and harbour of Porthmadog. He had achieved this by buying, in 1798, a local estate which comprised the estuary of the river Glaslyn, and thereafter by successfully promoting two Acts of Parliament in 1807 and 1821. By these means he was enabled to build an embankment across the estuary of the Glaslyn and to reclaim many square miles of land in the tidal estuary. The town and harbour of Porthmadog were built on this reclaimed land, which passed into W. A. Maddocks's private ownership and became known as the Tremadog estate. The firm of Breese, Jones and Casson were the Tremadog estate solicitors and Edward Breese was the firm's principal when Myrddin Fardd brought Richard Lloyd and David to see him in his office in the summer of 1878, with a view to finding out whether he could give David, then fifteen, a job in the office. Edward Breese was highly respected by the Porthmadog public on account of his fairness and ability. He was a Liberal and a Churchman.

He agreed to accept David for a trial period of six months from

July 1878 and said that if he took to the law during that time, he would arrange for him to be articled to Randall Casson, one of his partners. It was arranged that he should lodge at Porthmadog during week-days and return home to Llanystumdwy on Sundays. Because of David's age, Breese agreed to take a personal interest in his welfare and to keep an eye on him. David was encouraged to call at his house, Morfa Lodge, and indeed David's small diary, 'Diary of the Calvinistic Methodists 1878' bought in his first week in the office, contains daily entries from July onwards, many of them recording visits to Morfa Lodge.

David's entry into this office, at a time when Porthmadog was expanding and the town and harbour bustling with activity, was one of those strokes of good fortune without which his career would have taken an entirely different course. Moreover Edward Breese was an active and enthusiastic Liberal when it was unusual for a solicitor to be a Liberal, and he had acted as agent for the Liberal candidate in neighbouring Merioneth.

At this stage Richard Lloyd and David Lloyd George may well have remembered that William George was a great admirer of Henry Clay, the American statesman who had started out as an office boy in an attorney's office. David would perhaps have looked again at his father's notebooks with extracts from Clay's writings and thought of the future.

A more famous family hero was Abraham Lincoln who was held out to David as a great man whose example he might well emulate. And indeed throughout his life Lloyd George considered him one of the greatest men who had ever lived. David was entering on the law as a profession at a time when the underprivileged still tended to think of a lawyer as a knave or a swindler. By starting life as a lawyer Lincoln had done more than anyone to make the lawyer's profession respectable in the eyes of the common man. Lincoln himself was aware of the prejudice against the legal profession, and his words on this subject were a great encouragement to David at the time:

There is a vague popular belief that lawyers are necessarily dishonest. I say vague because when we consider to what extent confidence and honors are reposed in and conferred upon lawyers by the people, it appears improbable that their impression of dishonesty is very distinct and vivid. Yet the impression is common—almost universal. Let no young man choosing the law for a calling for a moment yield to this popular belief. Resolve to be honest at all events; and if, in your judgment, you cannot be an honest lawyer, resolve to be honest without being a lawyer.

79

These words and the examples of both Lincoln and Clay were quite an influence in the choice of the law as a career for David and William. And so strong was the admiration for Lincoln in our family that I myself was brought up to hero-worship him.

When he started keeping his diary on 8 July 1878 David Lloyd George laid down three guide-lines for himself and initialled each of them:

Those who talk much cannot but talk some nonsense.·. Be they as wise as ever—Talk little but to the purpose.

D.Ll.G.

If I were to talk less in Bible class, but that the little I talked should be always good and right, they would listen more to what I said and respect me more.

D.Ll.G.

In office don't show yourself knowing or they will think you dogmatic —or a conceited fool.

D.Ll.G.

He recorded that he didn't sleep at all his first night, and his entry for his first full day from home reads:

1878
July 9, Tues. *Codi* ½ past 4 a.m. [Got up 4.30 a.m.] Morfa Lodge [i.e. Edward Breese's home]. With W. Owen copying. Walk M. E. George [his sister] here. Mr. Breese not in office.
July 11, Thurs. Went to meet M. E. George in station, she going to station. Brings my law book with her. Read till 8 p.m. Dull (Lodge).
July 12, Fri. Reading in a.m. Morfa Lodge. Walk past Penamser and Tremadog with J. R. and W. Lloyd Arthur. Gladstone eastern question—Republic; aristocracy. Read till 7. 26.

The law book he refers to was Williams's *Real Property*, of which he made a detailed synopsis at the end of his diary.

These early entries refer to almost daily visits to Morfa Lodge and to meeting, and sometimes going for a long walk with, John Roberts. He was a member of the Porthmadog chapel of the same denomination as the Criccieth chapel of which David was a member. Uncle Lloyd may have asked him to keep an eye on David. He certainly did so and it was in his dimly lit shed, whilst he was making tallow candles for the Blaenau Ffestiniog quarries, that David heard really radical opinions being voiced for the first time. My father, of course, remembered John Roberts and was in a better position than anyone in later years to assess his influence on David. This is his description:

The candle-house was situate in a by-street just behind the little chapel belonging to the denomination known as the 'Disciples of Christ', of which John Roberts was a deacon and in which he often preached. The candle-house was a popular meeting place for young people who liked to congregate once the day's work was over to discuss topics of popular interest, and Dafydd frequently joined them. John Roberts had very little that was good to say of either of the two great parties of those days, the Tory and Liberal parties. 'A plague on both your houses' would be the phrase to describe his feelings towards them. He would declaim at length on the extravagance of the Royal Family and the corruption of the 'idle rich'. When I think of the seeds scattered around in that dimly lit tallow-shed, I cannot help wondering how many of them found fertile ground in the heart of the young lawyer to be.*

The first written reference Lloyd George ever made to a political question is the reference to Gladstone and the Eastern question in the diary entry I have just quoted. Gladstone spoke of 1878 as a 'tumultuous year'. In the summer the famous congress assembled at Berlin (13 June to 13 July) with Disraeli and Lord Salisbury representing the Tory government. It is a highly significant diary entry, in my view, inasmuch as it reveals precisely the topics of popular interest John Roberts and his friends were discussing with Lloyd George in the candle-house and on their long walks. Lloyd George was at an impressionable age. He heard John Roberts praising Gladstone with the fervour of an evangelical preacher for his courage and high moral principle in coming out of his retirement to conduct a campaign to arouse the conscience of his fellow countrymen against the policy of the Tory government which was supporting the Turks and thereby condoning the Bulgarian horrors (May 1876), when some 12,000 Christians in Bulgaria had been murdered by irregular Turkish troops. In his *History of Europe*,† H. A. L. Fisher states, in reference to Gladstone's campaign:

The campaign which he then conducted in and out of Parliament is one of the outstanding physical and oratorical achievements in English history.

Gladstone's one-man crusade against the Turks because of the Bulgarian atrocities had shown great moral courage, when popular feeling throughout the country was running high in favour of going

* *My Brother and I*, William George, Eyre & Spottiswoode, 1958, pp. 110–11.
† Arnold, 1936, p. 1043.

to war against Russia; the idea that the Russian bear would soon be rent by the British lion was so popular that it was difficult in any part of the country, particularly London, to attempt to hold a meeting in favour of peace. Nevertheless Gladstone's sustained campaign had aroused the conscience of the majority of the working class, the great majority of church and chapel members and intellectuals, such as Ruskin and Carlyle, against the idea of the projected war. This Eastern problem had, largely due to Gladstone's campaign, just been peaceably resolved at Berlin when David Lloyd George made this, his first extant reference to a major political issue.

Lloyd George's early diary entries from 1878 onwards contain frequent, sometimes daily, references to John Roberts, who, with his friends introduced Lloyd George at the early age of fifteen and a half to the Porthmadog Debating Society. He decided to speak on the Eastern question and the notes for this, the first speech he ever made, have survived in his articled-clerk's handwriting. He had obviously heard the well-known refrain, sung in London music-halls by the war party:

> *We don't want to fight,*
> *But by Jingo, if we do,*
> *We've got the men, we've got the ships,*
> *We've got the money too.*

He said:

Let us grant for an instance that the young men, who conducted the late Jingo agitation were in possession of that 'engine of power', the electoral franchise, combined with that minority of the property-class, which was led away by such phantasms,—they might have plunged this country into war. Having committed ourselves to the trammels of the complicated relations and the varied and numerous interests which the Eastern question involved,—Heaven knows what and where would be the terminus. Who is it that would have to bear the costs of such a war and suffer in case the war proved disastrous to our cause,— in case the fortune of war sided with our foes, were our ships to be destroyed by the piratical flotillas of Russia, and what is not beyond the bounds of possibility,—were our coasts to be invaded by a victorious foe.

Youth are easily enticed and led away by the 'gunpowder and glory business'. It tickles their fancy and pleases their imagination.

Although republicanism was not a prominent issue generally in 1878, it was nevertheless discussed in the candle-shed, particularly with reference to the undeserved status of the privileged few, the

82

aristocracy. The discussions in the candle-shed were the rehearsals
for the real thing in the Porthmadog Debating Society meetings.
My uncle made numerous notes in preparation for these debates,
and one note he made explains the thinking behind the diary
reference to 'Republic; aristocracy':

Material for Speech on Republicanism

Monarchy's regalia pleasing to the fancy—Toys please children, in
body or mind or both, but before you titillate your drivelling (doting)
lunatics or imbeciles (simpletons) don't you think it would be better
to feed your starving paupers?

*　　*　　*

Some persons tell us that if ever we get protection that prosperity
will mark our trade, but before we get real prosperity, before we can
thrive we must take privilege from the mansion of the great and
establish justice in the cottage of the humble.

These notes show that the author of the People's Budget (1909)
had formulated and expressed the principle upon which it was
based before he was twenty and whilst he was still a solicitor's
articled clerk in Porthmadog. In the past too great a formative
influence has been placed on the discussions in the village smithy
in Llanystumdwy or in Richard Lloyd's workshop; the contemporary records indicate that the first eighteen months or so David
Lloyd George spent as an articled clerk in Porthmadog were probably the most crucial in his development as a politician and statesman. He obviously enjoyed his freedom from the constraints of
life in the cottage at Llanystumdwy, and his mother gave him a
small weekly cash allowance, out of which he paid 10s a week to
Mrs. Owen, his landlady. The fact that he was fending for himself
at this early age must have helped him in maturing sooner than
many young men of his generation. Morcover, as the diary entries
reveal, he was obviously allowed to go for occasional walks with
girl-friends, without being under the surveillance later diary entries
show he was subject to, after the family had moved to Criccieth
and David once more was under the same roof as Uncle Lloyd.
Uncle Lloyd did not at this or any other period appear to David
as an ogre, from whose grasp he was glad to escape. Each Sunday
he recorded his admiration of Uncle Lloyd's sermons. The following entries are representative of most of his references:

1878
Sun. 1 Sept. Dull. Close. Baptism—Rob Davies & Judith in sea
shore. Uncle speaking splendid, 100's of people, nice Baptism. Everybody quiet and listening. *Brolio* [praising] Uncle.

83

Sun. 22 Sept. R. Lloyd (2). Splendid. *Efengyl gyntaf yn Ewrop.*
[Gospel first in Europe.]

Sun. 17 Nov. R. Lloyd. His climax splendid,—conversational and
then grand.

The fact that Uncle Lloyd had such a great influence over him
added to the significance of these months at Porthmadog; he was
for most of this time free to experience what life was like, away
from his uncle's direct sway. My father never had the experience
of leaving home at this early age, and I believe he accepted that it
was his lot in life to stay with Uncle Lloyd and to look after him
when he could no longer carry on with his work as a shoemaker.
But David on the other hand had this early taste of freedom and
the experience may have completely altered his outlook towards
life and his relationship with his family, which until then had been
so closely knit.

Throughout the period he exercised great self-discipline, getting
up between six and seven and sometimes even earlier each morning.
His first task was to take the letters from the office up the hill to
Mr. Breese's house, which occupies a fine position overlooking the
town, the harbour and the Glaslyn Estuary. He soon became
almost a member of the family, was invited to stay for meals—
including Christmas dinner—and he spent many carefree hours
playing with the Breese children in the grounds of Morfa Lodge.
Occasionally Mr. Breese dictated letters to him, but Lloyd George
was very unhappy that he couldn't improve the quality of his
handwriting and he tried out three or four different styles in this,
his first diary. He was on one occasion entrusted with a mortgage
deed which he was asked to engross. As the following comment
shows, he could be pointedly self-critical on occasion:

1878
Sept. 3 Dull. My mortgage *blêr* [untidy] ought to be better. Indeed,
I must, I WILL (D.V.) REFORM. *Crwydro trwy'r* p.m. [wandering through-
out the afternoon] looking for builders saying their leases are ready.

As I explained, Breese, Jones & Casson were the solicitors for
the Tremadog estate, who developed the land reclaimed from the
sea by laying out streets, which are a model of good town-planning,
and then leasing building plots to local builders on long-term
leases at a low rent, on condition that a house was built on each
plot to an approved plan within a stipulated period—usually
twelve months. At the end of the lease, and some of the terms in
old leases I have seen were as short as sixty years, the plot of land
and the house reverted to the ownership of the landlords. In fair-

ness to the Tremadog estate it should be remembered that they did not apply the full rigour of the leasehold system against the tenants, but sold the reversions on reasonable terms to the lessees. The result is that there are probably more freehold owner-occupied houses in Porthmadog today than in almost any comparable town. Nevertheless at this office Lloyd George was to see the leasehold system in operation from the landlord's side, and he was fortunate that the firm's principals were Liberals who operated the system on behalf of the estate in a progressive and enlightened manner. There is nothing in Lloyd George's diary entries to indicate that he was critical of the system; he probably did not see any evidence of its abuse under Mr. Breese's just and fair treatment of the builders and tenants.

Lloyd George disciplined himself rigorously over his spare-time reading. He set himself a daily target and frequently recorded the number of pages he had read on a particular day as he worked his way through Williams on Real Property, his first major legal reading. When he had finished Williams he read some Shakespeare. His father's library included Shakespeare's complete works in Knight's Cabinet Edition, published in 1843, and these pocket-sized volumes provided a never failing source of reading material for both brothers. Shakespeare, however, was a temporary diversion. The young Lloyd George knew that he must get back to the law, at any rate for the next few years and the entry for 23 October 1878 shows his next choice:

1878
Oct. 23 In Police station a.m. hearing Arbitration case; and after 5 o'clock p.m. till 7 o'clock then read Hallam, which I brought with me from home.

Hallam consisted of two leather-bound volumes—*The Constitutional History of England*, published by John Murray in 1842. His father had bought the volumes second-hand, probably at one of the London bookshops he frequented during his stay there. For the next few weeks, the diary entries show that Lloyd George, not yet sixteen, tackled this heavy-going reading with persistence, and the part of the work dealing with the constitution of Ireland has several marginal pencil notes. He made use of passages from Hallam in preparing his notes for his speeches in the Porthmadog and Criccieth Debating Societies. The opening sentences of the second volume may have effectively countered the influence of John Roberts's republican sympathies on his mind, and helped to make Lloyd George a supporter of the monarchy for the rest of his life:

It is universally acknowledged that no measure was ever more national, or has ever produced more testimonies of public approbation, than the restoration of Charles II. Nor can this be attributed to the usual fickleness of the multitude. . . . The king's return seemed to the people the harbinger of a real liberty, instead of that bastard commonwealth, which had insulted them with its name.

During these early months in Porthmadog Lloyd George was laying down for himself, often deliberately and with remarkable prescience, an attitude towards the world and its affairs which was to remain with him throughout life. Even before he started reading Hallam in earnest, there is nothing to suggest that he was impressed by the republican argument; for instance on 18 September he records:

D. Ll. Owen [his landlady] went very saucy and *brwnt* [nasty] because I was late in house; in W. Davies' house with W.A.Ll; talk about Republic, of the same opinion as me.

The internal evidence points to Lloyd George being late in returning to his lodgings, after he had taken part in a lengthy discussion in which he had differed from the candle-shed republican opinion, as expounded by John Roberts.

In addition to his daily readings of Hallam he also started attending shorthand classes during 1878 and 1879. He writes:

1878
8 Oct. Tues. Mr. Holl; had first shorthand lesson in house [of] W. Jones. I am (D.V.) going to try shorthand—a long pull and a good pull.

He did in fact learn sufficient shorthand to keep most of his 1880 diary in it—shorthand which experts find difficult to transcribe today. My father also learnt shorthand and kept his diaries for many years almost entirely with it.

Lloyd George was existing on an exceedingly slender budget at this period. The allowance he had from home was supplemented by the commission he earned in calling on Porthmadog householders to collect industrial insurance premiums, which were paid weekly through the agency of Mr. Holl, his shorthand teacher. At the end of the week he was lucky if he still had four shillings left in his purse. On 12 November he recorded that he received 15s of Mr. Holl for collecting insurance; he added—'bought cakes'. Though Mr. Breese invited him to have Christmas dinner with him at Morfa Lodge, Lloyd George spent his Christmas Day in 1878 at home. Two of the deacons of the Criccieth church,

William Williams and his cousin G. P. Williams, called at Highgate: 'Had 6d of W.W. and splendid knife of G.P.W. How kind.'
As far as I know these were his only Christmas gifts, but by the
end of the year Lloyd George had convinced his principals that he
was in earnest as an embryo lawyer and should be admitted to five
years of articled clerkship, before he could qualify as a fully fledged
solicitor. It was arranged that he should be articled as soon as
possible after his sixteenth birthday on 17 January 1879 to Randall
Casson, one of the partners.

It is interesting to note that when he was entering on his articles
he put a few questions to himself:

Q. *Your chief ambition?* A. *To promote myself by honest endeavour to
benefit others.*

Q. *The noblest aim in life.* A. *(1) To develop our manhood. (2) To do
good. (3) To seek truth. (4) To bring truth to benefit our fellows.*

Q. *Your idea of Happiness.* A. *To perceive my own efforts succeed.*

In one of his notebooks Lloyd George's father had commented:

Enterprise, confidence, a disposition to believe that good can be done
—these constitute important elements in the character of every man
who is of use to the world. We want no wailing or whimpering about
the absence of happiness, but a steady determination to abate misery.
. . . The endeavour to promote the happiness of others increases our
own.

Lloyd George's replies to his own questions clearly echo these
reflections noted by his father, who had been influenced by the
principles of moral philosophy enunciated by Locke and developed
by the freethinker Bentham, particularly the view that the general
happiness is the *summum bonum* and the theory that it is the business
of laws and institutions to maintain an equitable balance between
the public good and personal self-advancement. This theory was
so attractive and noted by Lloyd George in his notes so frequently
that in time its application in practice shaped the nature and
directed the course of his own political career. To alleviate in
some measure the misery suffered by millions of his fellow human
beings was the dominant aim of his political life. Although he
emerged into prominence in Wales as a champion of an oppressed
minority, it should always be recognized that from the beginning
the mainspring of his political actions was to put into practice in
the social life of the country the principle of moral philosophy
which he had read at the impressionable age of sixteen in his
deceased father's notebook.

CHAPTER SIX

THE LAW AND POLITICS

Another early note by Lloyd George declares:

Most admired character in real life—Michael Davitt.
Statesmen—Gladstone—Chamberlain & Parnell.

This note indicates the political personalities who appealed to the young Lloyd George. It is necessary to know something of the political climate in Wales and particularly in the county of Merioneth during the second half of the last century to appreciate why they should have done so. The note is undated, but was made in his 'articled clerk's' handwriting, and clearly before the split, which occurred later in the 1880s, between Gladstone and Chamberlain over the Irish Home Rule issue.

The years between 1850 and 1865 had not seen in Wales any real expression of the revolutionary spirit which had erupted in Europe in 1848. The awakening of national consciousness amongst the Welsh people was a very slow and gradual process. One reason for which was the tenant-farmers' deep-seated and generations-old fear of their landlords. The tenant-farmers of Merioneth in particular had been browbeaten into submission by their landlords during these years. County landlords had been returned unopposed as Tory candidates between 1837 and 1859, but in 1859 David Williams, the founder of Breese, Jones and Casson, was prevailed upon to stand as a Liberal candidate against W. W. E. Wynne, the sitting Tory member. The landed aristocracy of Merioneth came out strongly in favour of Wynne and Richard Watkin Price, a landlord with an extensive estate in Merioneth, sent the following letter to each of his tenants: 'Mr. —, You will do me a favour by voting for Mr. Wynne in the forthcoming election.'* Wynne himself sent his estate manager to Bala to warn his tenants of the perils of not voting in his favour. The election was an open election, and the landlords would know how each of their tenants had voted. The threats worked and Wynne was returned by a narrow majority of twenty votes.

Amongst the evictions which followed the refusal of some

* See *Cofiant Thomas Gee*, T. Gwynn Jones, Gee 1913, Vol. 1, p. 204.
88

tenants to vote for Wynne, was that of Edward Ellis by the Tory candidate himself. Edward Ellis was the uncle of Thomas Edward Ellis, who was born in the election year of 1859 and was destined to come into prominence as a Welsh national leader on his election to Parliament as Liberal member for Merioneth in 1886. The political persecution of the tenant-farmers of Merioneth following the open-voting election in 1859 was a major cause of the awakening of the political conscience of Wales; this awakening expressed itself in the 1868 election—the last of the open-voting elections, when David Williams was elected as Liberal M.P. for Merioneth and Love Jones-Parry won Caernarfonshire for the Liberals against G. Douglas Pennant, the son and heir of Lord Penrhyn, owner of the famous quarries in Bethesda.

Another major factor in arousing the nonconformist conscience in Wales was the impression created by the American Civil War. The speeches of Bright, Cobden, Lincoln and Ward Beecher proclaimed not only the wrongs of slavery but also the tyranny of depriving men of their basic civil liberties. Welsh people had already emigrated in appreciable numbers to the United States on account of the civil oppression to which they were subjected at home and the lack of any prospect for material advancement for themselves and their families under the conditions of grinding poverty which faced them on the upland farms of their homeland. In fact, before the 1859 election, under the leadership of Michael D. Jones of Bala, a movement was launched to found a Welsh colony in Patagonia. Jones's plan was to found the colony amongst the Patagonian Indians on the model of the colony founded by William Penn amongst the American Indians. He hoped that they would become a self-governing province under the Argentine government. In furtherance of his project Jones travelled extensively in the United States; his dream was to persuade up to 30,000 Welsh emigrés, scattered in different parts of the United States to combine with Welshmen emigrating direct from Wales in founding a strong and self-supporting independent Welsh nation on Patagonian soil. He feared that Welshmen were spread so thinly over the vast expanse of the States that they would in time lose their identity as Welshmen. His efforts met with only partial success and the first pioneers to land in Patagonia in 1865 had to spend several days and nights in caves and makeshift shelters on an exposed, inhospitable shore, short of food and drink. But the story of the movement to found a Welsh and Welsh-speaking colony in Patagonia has an epic quality about it. It was a great vision by several Welsh leaders of the mid-nineteenth century, which the injustices of the 1859 election brought to the point of action.

The venture did not fully succeed, partly on account of insufficient support in terms both of manpower and money which Jones had hoped would have been forthcoming from both Wales and the United States. Unfortunately several ships carrying essential cargo were wrecked, and others were arrested on one pretext or another by the Argentine government. This made a bad impression both at home and in the States. A more fundamental oversight by the founding fathers was that Welsh people, who either in the first or second generation had already uprooted themselves by emigrating to the United States, were unlikely to be prepared to emigrate for a second time—unless the clearest proof existed that it would be to their positive and lasting advantage to do so. The emigration to Patagonia from Wales was a political act, a political protest against the injustice experienced by the Welsh tenant farmer and quarryman and the denial of his right to the official use of his language. It would be wrong to dismiss the movement as a form of escapism; it succeeded to the extent that a Welsh-speaking colony was, in fact, founded in the teeth of almost superhuman difficulties, and that even today an appreciable number of Spanish and Welsh-speaking descendants of the 1865 pioneers live and work in Patagonia. They are citizens of the Argentine Republic, but many of them have close family links with their homeland in Wales. In later years David Lloyd George was to make a voyage to South America in connection with a Welsh-Patagonian gold-mining company's affairs; this company was not a success, but it played a significant part in the attempt by Lloyd George to endow himself with the worldly goods of which he was woefully short at the beginning of his professional and political career.

The servitude of the Welsh people at this period was closely linked with the inferior status of their language. The irony of the situation was that Welsh-speaking people had themselves come to regard the use of their language as a mark of inferiority. There is an illustration of this social attitude in an article in the January 1895 issue of a Welsh monthly periodical, *Geninen*. It refers to the experience of two Welsh authors of the mid-nineteenth century, who had walked up Snowdon in the company of a Welsh guide. The two authors spoke English throughout their walk up the mountain; it was considered fashionable to do so, but on arriving at the summit they were both so overcome by the magnificence of the view that they gave vent to their feelings in Welsh, their mother tongue. The Welsh guide could not conceal his dismay and appeared to be on the verge of tears: 'You're Welsh,' he exclaimed, 'I had all along thought you were two *gentlemen*!'

90

Whatever Welshmen may feel today concerning the fate of their language, the young Lloyd George of 1880 was, as his note at the beginning of this chapter indicates, more interested in the return to power of a Liberal government under Gladstone's premiership in that year, following the historic Midlothian campaign. On 14 March 1880, Gladstone had written to Lord Acton:

On Tuesday I am to set out for Midlothian and my *last* general election. My general elections have been 1832, 1835, 1837, 1841, 1847, 1852, 1859, 1865, 1868, 1874 and now 1880—what a list!

No wonder Lloyd George had named Gladstone first amongst his list of statesmen. In 1880 Lord Beaconsfield and the Tories were swept out of office. The Liberals under Gladstone's premiership were once more in power. What an important year this was for Lloyd George. Parnell, an Irish Protestant and landowner, had entered Parliament in 1875 and in the five years between 1875 and 1880 had established himself as the leader of the Irish peasantry. In the new Parliament of 1880 he was elected chief of the Home Rule party. The Irish Land League, founded by Michael Davitt in 1879, was already a force in the land. In 1880, 10,000 evictions took place in Ireland and a corresponding number of agrarian outrages were provoked as a direct consequence of these acts of injustice. Gladstone's humanitarian instincts as a Christian and Liberal statesman were deeply involved; he declared: 'My mission is to pacify Ireland.'

During a previous administration in 1869, under Gladstone's premiership, the Irish Church Act had been passed. This measure not only completely severed the Protestant Episcopal Church in Ireland from the established Church of England but it also provided for the distribution of some sixteen millions of the Irish Church's endowments among institutions—'not for the maintenance of any church or clergy, nor for the teaching of religion, but mainly for the relief of unavoidable calamity and suffering'. This Act led to a demand amongst nonconformists in Wales that the Church of England in Wales should be treated in a similar manner and disestablished. Gladstone was asked by Welsh Liberal M.P.s in 1870 to grant Wales religious equality with Ireland, but he firmly opposed the proposal. He said the established Church in Wales, of which he was a lay pillar, possessed 'a complete constitutional, legal and historical identity with the Church of England'. Welsh Liberal M.P.s were themselves divided on the issue, but Thomas Gee, a promiment Welsh radical and journalist, who took a leading part in forming and activating Welsh nonconformist opinion for over half a century, prophesied that Gladstone 'would live to eat his words'.

There were two parliamentary elections during 1880 in Caernarfonshire. The first was the General Election at the beginning of April, when the seat was won by Watkin Williams (Liberal), a barrister who gained a substantial majority over his opponent, G. Douglas Pennant. The second was a bye-election held in November. The General Election campaign involved Lloyd George in political activity for the first time. Not only did he help to check the election registers—a practical exercise of great use to him ten years later— but he assisted in canvassing on behalf of the Liberal candidate and attended political meetings at Caernarfon, Criccieth and Porthmadog. Welsh affairs were to the fore at both election campaigns, and Lloyd George was fortunate to have been articled at the office of Breese, Jones & Casson, the Liberal agents, at this crucial period in the awakening of his political interests.

He has the following references to the March election in his diary:

1880

Tues. 9 March Dull but fine. News of a dissolution of Parliament comes.

Tues. 16 Fine. Watkin Williams with 4.30 train. Splendid reception. He made a speech at Town Hall. Very good, but nothing brilliant. A very good meeting throughout. *Stephens Commentaries*, little in morning. [*Stephens Commentaries* was the standard legal textbook to be read in preparation for the Intermediate examination of the Law Society for which Lloyd George was studying.]

Wed. 17 Dull. To Llandecwyn with Edwards, canvassing. Know nothing of country. We would get more than we might have done with knowledge of the country. [Llandecwyn is in Merioneth for which constituency Mr. Breese was also the Liberal agent.]

Thurs. 18 Very fine. Off with first train in morning. Canvassing all day. Very hurried. Home with last train. Out with Mary Lloyd.

Fri. 19 Fine. With 11.30 train, Mr. Jones and self canvassing. Home with last train.

Sat. 20 Very fine. Went with John Caerdyni who was here, up to Prenteg to see someone about his vote. Home with 5.30 train. To Criccieth with Uncle. Willie my brother sick.

Mon. 22 Very fine. To Port with 8.20 train. Up to Ffestiniog with 1.15 train, serving some notices. Down with 6 train. Splendid scenery along the line to Ffestiniog.

1a Highgate, Llanystumdwy

1b Capel Ucha, Criccieth

2a William George,
Lloyd George's father

2b Elizabeth George,
Lloyd George's mother

3a Richard Lloyd

3b William George,
Lloyd George's brother

4a Lloyd George
at the age of sixteen

4b Margaret Owen,
circa 1882

5a Llanystumdwy Bridge

5b The Porthmadog office of Lloyd George & George

6a David Evans,
Llanystumdwy schoolmaster

6b Randall Casson

6c Michael Davitt

6d Michael Jones of Bala

7a View of Criccieth, *circa* 1880

7b Llanfrothen Church

8 Lloyd George in 1890

Wed. 24 Fine. Went to Talsarnau with a Methodist Minister. Saw some of the voters and attended a committee at Penrhyn. Home with car.—Mr. Casson, Edwards & others. Had supper Edwards & I with Mr. Casson.

Thurs. 25 Fine but cloudy. To Penrhyn sessions with 11.30 train. Nothing scarcely to do. Went up to Llanfrothen with Mr. Casson with the intention of canvassing, but voters all in vestry. Came down along the Glaslyn in a boat. Home with last train.

Fri. 26 Dull. With my brother through morning. In Criccieth p.m. with my sister and brother. Went to see proposed new house. To Caerdyni. Annie & Jennie came there. I went to Criccieth with John. Saw the girls afterwards. Was reserved with Jennie. I want to get rid of her—we are being talked about. Uncle knows it this long time!

Sat. 27 Fine. To Port with 8.20 train. Douglas Pennant here. A most insulting reception, carrying effigy before him with red herrings in its mouth (it was two-faced) and rabbit skins on its arms! To Criccieth in car with Davies, Police Station. Pennant was there. Meeting was mixed. Gwynfryn ladies there, but his reception not at all good. Saw Jennie there—took scarcely any notice of her. Avoided her. Walk with Uncle.

Mon. 29 Fine. At Mr. Jones' request on Saturday with 8.20 train. Jennie here; avoided her. Mary Ellen and brother here in p.m. Went to cover. It costs me some trouble to get rid of that girl, but in flirting with her, I have everything to lose and nothing to win. This shall be regarded as proof of my pluck. If I cannot resist this, how do I expect to gain other things, which require a good deal more determination. She attempted to tease me by flirting with others—bastards.

Thurs. 1 April News of the first Liberal victories. Am glad. It is very likely that they will carry everything before them now.

Sat. 3 Dull day. *Stephens Commentaries* 143–160. Learnt chapter for Sunday school. Liberal victories splendid. Kenealy out. Half glad. He was an egoistic, self-sufficient fanatic. Home with 4 train. Walk with Uncle. He gave me a speech he had prepared to deliver at a Liberal meeting, but, of course, he never in fact did so. It was splendid, spicy, epigrammatic.

Sun. 4 Unsettled, cloudy, showers. The suspense and anxiety as to yesterday's polling painful, but for news of Liberal victories at Flint and Anglesey.

Mon. 5 Showery. . . . News that Gladstone in for Midlothian. Great enthusiasm here.

D

Wed. 7 Weather fine. Polling in Merionethshire. News in p.m. that Watkin Williams got in for Caernarfonshire. Scenes of wildest enthusiasm. Evan butcher got hold of donkey that was passing and shouted in its ears that its brother had lost! Bonfires and fire-balls. Out till 10 to twelve with Mary Lloyd. The victory beyond the most sanguine expectations. Figures—3303 Williams, 2206 Pennant. A great blow to landlord terrorism, and quite as great a triumph for the ballot. *Stephens' Commentaries*, few pages. News that night Holland (Liberal) in for Merioneth, 800 majority. A good row here in the night to celebrate return of Holland.

Fri. 9 . . . Out till 11.30 expecting results of N.E. Lancs. Hartington and Grafton in—two Liberal candidates. The Liberal victory throughout the kingdom increasing—16 yesterday.

After little more than six months as Member for Caernarfonshire Watkin Williams accepted a judgeship at the end of October 1880 and a bye-election was held. The campaigning took place during November. The Liberal candidate on this occasion was William Rathbone, a Liverpool businessman. He had little sympathy with Welsh aspirations. His Conservative opponent was H. J. Ellis-Nanney of Gwynfryn, the Llanystumdwy squire whom Lloyd George was to oppose and defeat by eighteen votes in another Caernarfonshire bye-election in 1890. In the meantime Lloyd George, when he heard that 'Watkin Williams has accepted judgeship', recorded in his diary: 'Election—delighted.' This entry and the earlier entries recording his suspense, whilst awaiting the election results in April 1880, show that he was personally and emotionally involved in politics at the age of seventeen, before he had even sat his intermediate Law Society examination. On 1 November 1880, after reading *Stephens Commentaries*, pp. 530–5, and 'taking some notes', he sent a letter to the *North Wales Express* under the pseudonym of 'Brutus'. Its subject was a speech by the Marquis of Salisbury at Taunton. Its final paragraph compared the Toryism of Canning favourably with that of Salisbury, because 'Toryism had not been barren of statesmen', who had rendered laudable assistance, in the name of England, to 'weak nationalities in their desperate struggles for Liberty—for freedom from the yoke of inhuman despots—for very existence'. These were comments of almost prophetic relevance by a seventeen-year-old Porthmadog articled clerk. At the time he had his doubts as to whether the editor would publish his letter; 'after sending it off, I am not free from contrition for a rather hasty act. Do not relish that refusal, which editor overwhelmed with a redundance of such trash will have to accord to some of them.' In fact, his letter was published 'on same page as leading article'. It was, he recorded with satisfaction, his 'first attempt of this kind'.

Encouraged by the reception accorded to his first article, Lloyd George records in his diary:

1880
Tues. 16 Nov. Cold. Hail. Stormy. Sea is a magnificent sight, sublime in the waves, beautiful in the spray. Wrote long letter on Mr. Nanney's address and sent it to *North Wales Express*. Am afraid its length, and I suspect its virulence, will tend to its exclusion. However, it does not matter much. It contains a severe—but not too severe attack upon Mr. Nanney. Read 9 or 10 pages of *Stephens Commentaries*.

Wed. 17 Cold. Went with 4 train to Criccieth. Mr. Rathbone there, very enthusiastic considering that it is regarded as the stronghold of Toryism. We had the intelligentsia of Criccieth to welcome Mr. Rathbone. A good meeting. There was one disturber, but his partisanship was banal—it counted for nothing, and Dr. John Thomas soon settled him by suggesting he was one of those people attending meetings with more in his belly than in his head. Had a lift on top of Morfa Lodge carriage with Bob Davies (Rathbone inside) to Portmadoc. Meeting there in Portmadoc, everybody there seemed to me to try and rival each other in talking nonsense. . . . Rathbone is a very poor orator though a sensible speaker. W. S. Caine, M.P. for Scarborough, present. My impression is that so far as speaking is concerned, the Welsh are incomparably superior to the English. They dragged Rathbone's carriage (I was not on it) all the way from Tremadoc to Portmadoc, and torch-bearers preceded and surrounded him,—altogether a most enthusiastic reception. Walked home from Portmadoc to Criccieth about mid-night. No *Stephens Commentaries*.

Thurs. 18 Very cold. Most piercing and incisive east wind. *Stephens Commentaries*, 13–25. Election time is not adopted for studying (politics nor anything else).

Fri. 19 Very cold. Most glad to see by the *North Wales Express* posters that there is 'An Address to Mr. Ellis Nanney by Brutus'. That 'gentleman' (?) was most honestly indignant that a truculent passage terming Mr. Nanney a vampire had been partially left out, and that the printer had made a few mistakes.

After castigating Ellis-Nanney for supporting a 'constitutional' Tory party, which had condoned or approved policies hostile to national minorities, particularly in Ireland, Lloyd George asks:

Does any good come out of Toryism? Are we to expect grapes from thorns, or figs of thistles? It is quite as preposterous an idea expecting beneficial measures from Conservatives.

Taking your past career to be any criterion of your future usefulness, your services may be safely declined until you have retrieved your parochial reputation. . . . You are just the man, whom the electors of Caernarfonshire would delight to reject with contumely.

Brutus.

Curiously enough the same issue of the *North Wales Express* reveals considerable support for Rathbone amongst Welsh landlords, including Frederick Wynn of Glynllifon, Caernarfonshire, a landlord of a vastly greater estate than Nanney's in Llanystumdwy. His letter does not attempt to deal with policy. He just says, 'I am glad to understand that you have determined to put the extinguisher on Mr. Nanney.' The combination of the traditional Whig vote, Welsh nonconformity and the Radical articles by 'Brutus' served to give Rathbone 3,080 votes against Nanney's 2,051, Lloyd George commented in his diary: 'As usual, some were disappointed and some elated, but on the whole, taking the potency of the cry of Race and Religion, I think we have every cause for congratulation. . . . I may say that Rathbone delivered a most effective speech from the balcony of the Castle Hotel and at the Pavilion, Caernarfon. This is a very large building, and the very sight of it stifles the aspirations of a young orator.' In later years Lloyd George was to deliver some of his most memorable speeches in this Pavilion.

By going to Caernarfon for the declaration of the poll, he missed the celebration of the Liberal victory in Porthmadog. He heard about it the following day and recorded in his diary:

1880

Thurs. 2 Dec. Hear that they had a splendid demonstration at Port. last night. Magnificent fireworks, mock-funeral—coffin borne with effigy of 'Last of the Tories' in procession, headed by band playing *Dead March in Saul*—too bad. Read but very few pages of *Stephens Commentaries*.

Sat. 4 Read up to page 123, i.e. 123 pages in weeks—average 60 pages a week. Creditable performance. Electioneering makes you neither a cool statesman nor a profound lawyer nor an ardent religionist (!)

His first-hand experience of two keenly contested elections made 1880 an important and memorable year for Lloyd George. But it was also the year in which the family left Highgate and became the tenants of Morvin House in Criccieth. It is an exceedingly pleasant terrace house, with ample accommodation, in contrast to the cramped conditions at Highgate, and has a superb view of mountain and sea from its front windows. They moved in May, and in addition to furniture and books, some gooseberry and fruit trees accompanied the family. Lloyd George was particularly proud of a royal fern, which he had found growing between the rocks overlooking the Dwyfor and planted in the garden at Highgate. This too was uprooted and replanted in the small garden at the back of Morvin House. It flourished there until my father built Garthcelyn in 1892, when it was transplanted there and continued to flourish until sometime after Lloyd George's Criccieth home, Bryn Awelon, was built in 1908. So great was the family's attachment to this royal fern that an attempt was made to divide it and transplant the uprooted half to the Bryn Awelon garden. Unfortunately both halves then languished and withered away. This caused considerable grief to both brothers. The royal fern was a living symbol of their boyhood in the village of Llanystumdwy, their attachment to the Dwyfor and its wooded banks and to a way of life, close to nature, which ceased to be theirs when they moved to Morvin House. My uncle's diary entries, at the time they moved, give no hint of the '*hiraeth*' (nostalgia) for Llanystumdwy, which was later to become rooted in his mind; in the closing months of his life this *hiraeth* was so strong that he expressly stated he did not wish to be buried in Westminster Abbey and chose a spot for a grave in the spinney overlooking the river, where he and his mates used to play soldiers during the Franco-Prussian War of 1870.

1880
Sun. 9 May Very nice day. Very hot. Sunday school. Recited chapter. Baptising day. R. Lloyd (2) splendid. W. Williams (6) good. A very lively singing meeting. Singing some anthems and cantatas which Ann Jones brought there. Sitting in the middle of girls—in the arm of Jennie ha-ha! To Llanystumdwy, and slept there for the last time, perhaps for ever.

Mon. 10 Dull. To Portmadoc with 8.20 train. Left Llanystumdwy without one feeling of regret, remorse nor longing. Read a little on some case which Mr. Casson gave me to study, but in no mood to study.

One of the first effects of the removal to Criccieth was that the freedom he had enjoyed as a Porthmadog lodger virtually came to an end. He continued staying at Porthmadog until the beginning of June. Two nights after arriving at Morvin House he records:

Sat. 5 June Home with 4 train. With John Caerdyni and others out

97

till 9.35 or so. Uncle thinks it late. Just a clue to what I am to expect when I come to stay at Criccieth.

Mon. 7 Saw Jennie. Talking for a good long time. Feel rather queer, something bordering on the unpleasant at first in the change, but believe it will be better ultimately, though much of what I may regard as liberty be curtailed.

He soon settled in to his lifelong habit of early rising—about six —and reading before breakfast. He frequently walked the five miles from Criccieth to Porthmadog, arriving in the office there at nine.

On 31 December 1880 Lloyd George recorded in his diary:

The present year is speedily flying to preterite eternity. . . . A retrospect of the past leaves everything but pleasant impressions. Its reminiscences are remorseful. The past is indelible, undeviable and unalterable. May the *future past* be a clear, unmistakable deflection from the *preterite* past. Ambition itself has had a greater sway in my thoughts than the means of its gratification. To my lasting shame be it said—Love can fairly record me amongst its infatuated brain-skinned devotees. *Stephens Commentaries*—My attention to this book might have been closer.

Lloyd George knew that he would have to do an immense amount of reading and memorizing if he were to stand a reasonable chance of passing the solicitors' intermediate examination. If he failed he knew the family's financial resources, already stretched to breaking point, could not possibly keep him under articles indefinitely. The allotted five years were long enough in all conscience. He knew that the sacrifice his mother was making could not be repeated for the benefit of William if he failed to win through. Bearing in mind how much depended on his passing his legal examinations he would be bound to feel guilty concerning any self-indulgence on his part which diverted him from his studies. Having no law-school to supervise his work, he realized that if he eventually failed, his failure would be due mainly to a lack of self-discipline in achieving the daily reading targets he set himself. He was a high-spirited youth with an abundance of natural vitality. He had realized early in life how attractive he was to women. It is obvious from his diary entries that he enjoyed his early flirtations and would have been prepared to echo the sentiment in the well-known verse:

> *O love, they wrong thee much*
> *Who say thy fruit is bitter,*
> *When thy ripe fruit is such*
> *That nothing could be sweeter.*

What deterred him from savouring the ripe fruit to the full was partly his awareness of the threat to his studies and ultimately his career that this self-indulgence could cause, and partly the open hostility of Uncle Lloyd to his goings-on. His sister, too, criticized him, and often he felt he had been unfairly attacked. For instance, in July 1880 he recorded:

We had no Singing Meeting—some of the songstresses could not attend. Do not mean to have any more of them. Read until 8.30— (Stephens) 293–309. Out with John Caerdyni—on top of Dinas. Splendid view. Feel quite as happy without being troubled as to whereabouts of any girls, though I have not courted with any of them. On good terms with all. It is when I have occasional fits of total abstention from girls that I am sometimes attacked ! !

The fit of 'total abstention' in July 1880 had apparently followed a particularly vigorous ticking-off by Uncle Lloyd and his sister the previous June:

15 June . . . went with the girls for walk along Marine Terrace, Jennie with me. We, both of us, went through Dinas home. Uncle gave it to me when I came back and told me I was becoming the town talk, that I must mend my ways in this matter, at least, or else it would ruin my chances of success.

17 June Hot and sultry. Up about 6 . . . My sister gave it to me rather solemnly for flirting with Jennie etc. Indeed I am rather disposed to give up these dealings. This I know—that the realization of my prospects, my dreams, my longings for success are very scant indeed, unless I am determined to give up what without mistake are the germs of a 'fast life'. . . . What is life good for unless some success, some reputable notoriety be attained—the idea of living merely for the sake of living is almost unbearable—it is unworthy of such a superior being as man.

Whilst his sister, and probably also Uncle Lloyd at that time, undoubtedly thought of Lloyd George's success in terms of his eventually passing his final examination and qualifying as a solicitor, he himself had become so interested in politics during the 1880 election campaigns that he had already set his sights much higher than achieving success as a prosperous country solicitor.

The first positive indication that Lloyd George was thinking of success in terms of becoming an internationally known statesman is contained in his diary entries referring to the death of General Garfield, the twentieth President of the United States. Garfield was a president in the Lincoln tradition, having been born in a log cabin and brought up in conditions of extreme poverty. Having worked for a time as a canal boatman, he eventually by dint of studying hard and developing his latent talent, became a leading politician and leader of the House of Representatives. He was the target of violent personal abuse on account of his alleged financial irregularities, but he weathered the storm and was inaugurated as President in March 1881. But on 2 July 1881 he was shot whilst at a railway station and died in September. He had been an ardent supporter of the anti-slavery campaign in America. Lloyd George referred to his feelings at Garfield's death as if he had sustained a personal bereavement:

1881

22 Sept. See by *Daily News* of y'day that Europe echoes with reports of his [Garfield's] good deeds. There is not to be found one paper running him down. The feeling throughout both Continents intense—There was never anything similar. For myself, I could not feel so much for any public man. Such is the influence of a good man. Is there not a hint of success here? Can he not be emulated? It is worth trying at any rate—The failure would not be ridiculous, because the intention would be too good to excite such commiseration.

27 Sept. Read in to-day's *Standard* the report of Garfield's funeral. There was a general sobbing—the little town of Cleveland overcrammed with real mourners. Never have I—never has anyone—heard of such general, deep mourning for any public man. Everyone seems to have lost a near relative. Shops closed; flags half-mast; bells tolled and muffled etc.

As I have mentioned already Abraham Lincoln was a firmly established hero in the eyes of Richard Lloyd and his family and Henry Clay had been highly regarded by Lloyd George's father; and when he thought of political success, Lloyd George was not thinking of the traditional British statesmen but of men like Clay, Lincoln and Garfield who had risen from the humblest origins to attain positions of supreme political power and influence. It was their example which inspired him to hope for great things in his own career. It is accordingly in the light of an already formed political ambition that Lloyd George's description of his first visit to the House of Commons should be read. He had gone up to London to sit his intermediate law examination in November 1881 and he knew that his future hinged on the outcome. Immediately after sitting the examination, he wrote:

There has been an admixture of hope and fear—hope predominating. I must now abide the result. If the verdict be adverse, I scarcely know what to do—to face friends and others who are so sanguine and seem

100

to have no doubt about the result will be terrible. I can scarcely conceive really the consequences of an adverse verdict. I will be disgraced—lowered in the estimation of my friends and gloated over by mine enemies.

During his stay in London he took the opportunity of seeing 'the principal places of interest' and some of his comments are interesting: '*Madame Tussauds*—The Chamber of Horrors. Oh! horror of horrors! I shall never go again.' '*Charing Cross Station:* Saw electric lighting (for the first time)—the light is a sort of pale blue —melancholy—but unquestionably stronger than gas.' '*The British Museum:* Interesting but too much of a good thing at a time—The mummies and handwritings are the most interesting features—Mr. Lloyd the Tremadoc parson there—He came up to me as I was contemplating the statue of Demosthenes.' '*St. Paul's:* An immense building; place not one-fourth full—the service was grand, the singing was the best I ever heard. In the evening left for Dr. Parker's. Place quite crammed. Slips with "FULL" printed thereon posted in front of building. However I got in and heard the Doctor; not an orator, at any rate not eloquent, —gesticulating too much and the features far from natural. A splendid voice.' '*At The Law Courts:* Q.Cs. are not perfect; they have a despicable cant—very garrulous.'

Sat. 12 Nov. Went to Houses of Parliament—very much disappointed with them. Grand buildings outside but inside they are crabbed, small and suffocating, especially House of Commons. I will not say but that I eyed the assembly in a spirit similar to that in which William the Conqueror eyed England on his visit to Edward the Confessor, the region of his future domain. Oh, vanity.

The news that Lloyd George had passed the examination was wired to Uncle Lloyd on 25 November. His own entry shows that he masterminded the method by which his two nephews studied:

More convinced than ever that our system is best. A thorough study of the whole—every book, chapter and note-text and footnotes— would rather been plucked [failed] after so doing than a superficial, cramming preparation under a primer 'to pass only'. [Translated from the Welsh.] Feel cause for gratitude that the boys have been so successful here without any external help—dedicated work on their own—steadiness—anxious to progress—May the Lord help them ever to be good boys and useful godly men—Let Him be thanked.

Uncle Lloyd was able to refer to the success of both his protégés because my father had sat and passed his preliminary law examination in May the year before. In the normal way, after passing this entrance examination to the profession, he would immediately have been admitted to his term of five years as an articled clerk, in the course of which he would sit both his intermediate and final examinations. William, however, was not admitted to articles following his success in passing the preliminary examination. Lloyd George had gone with his brother William to Beaumaris to keep an eye on him when he left home for the first time to sit this examination. David had grave doubts whether William would pass: 'Have some doubt whether Willie will pass. Could not prepare him myself owing to the distance to our then home.' In fact William passed the examination and Lloyd George made no reference at all to William in his daily diary entries until Friday 24 December 1880: 'Asked Mr. Breese whether he could get somewhere where Willie could be articled—promised to do his best—his office full at present.' When Lloyd George wrote in his diary at the end of 1880 that ambition itself had had greater sway in his thoughts than the means of its gratification, he probably realized that unless William were accepted into articles and eventually became a practising solicitor, he would find himself tied to earning his living as a solicitor on his own account and that it would be exceedingly difficult, if not impossible, for him to take up a political career without any financial backing. Members of Parliament were not then paid any salary.

William George was not in fact articled with the same firm of Porthmadog solicitors as his brother until 1882. Lloyd George underlined this fact in his diary, as it brought to an end a period of two years' uncertainty as to William George's future. Time after time the firm were approached to accept William but without success. Other firms of solicitors were approached with the same negative result, but Lloyd George persisted in asking. For instance he writes on 8 October 1881:

Asked Mr. Jones to-day if there be an opening sometime in their office if my brother had not in the meantime found an opening somewhere else, and whether he could promise me that W.G. would get the advantage of it. He said: 'Yes, I should be very glad of him, because you seem to me to be very good boys.' I thanked him for both the compliment and the promise.

28 Oct. T.J. told J.J. there was no present chance for admission to his office. Poor Will. Feel knocked out.

The T.J. in this entry was Thomas Jones, another Porthmadog solicitor, not the Jones of Breese, Jones & Casson. The brothers' cousin John had been to see Tom Jones in 1881 to ask if he had a vacancy for William George and when he was told that he was Lloyd George's brother, he asked, 'Is he as sharp as Lloyd George?' John replied that he was. Tom Jones commented: 'Lloyd George is a sharp little fellow' and promised to give his decision concerning William in a fortnight's time. Lloyd George wrote: 'William ought to abstain from procrastination. It has caused him an infinite amount of annoyance and some loss. Is it a fact really that people have a better opinion of him than he has of himself?'

Lloyd George's reference to William's procrastination indicates that William at this time was not so enthusiastic as his brother that he should become articled. Lloyd George was doing the running and William appeared to be holding back for he was not at all sure that he wanted to go in for the law. In a conversation they had about this period Lloyd George said he wanted to be a 'social reformer'; William had thoughts of becoming a doctor and like his father was interested in moral philosophy. He must have realized that once he was committed to the legal profession he could well be left to hold the baby, as his brother made no secret of his political ambitions. Lloyd George told William, in effect, that if he were to achieve his aim in life of being a great social reformer, he could not do so without his assistance. William accepted the challenge, and when he finally entered into his articles with Breese, Jones & Casson, he must have sensed that Lloyd George had had his way, and he accepted the situation, believing as he did throughout his life that it was part of the scheme of things, ordained by Providence, that he should fulfil this vital supporting role in the early stages of Lloyd George's career. Some of William's diary entries reveal what this decision meant to him in personal terms. At all events Lloyd George could see a clear path ahead from May 1882 on-wards, and fortunately Elizabeth George still had some of her late husband's building society's investments left to pay the stamp of £80 on the articles and the premium of £100 to Breese, Jones & Casson.

With his intermediate examination behind him and his younger brother securely committed to the solicitor's profession as his fellow articled clerk, Lloyd George decided to take life a little more easily during the summer of 1882. He co-operated with his brother in entering an essay competition on the subject of 'Cash & Credit' at the Criccieth Castle Festival in July and this proved to be the winning entry. Uncle Lloyd was not told until they announced to him that they had won and been paid the cash prize of £2 2s. He was quite elated, but said he would have stopped them from competing if he had known. Another of David Lloyd George's diversions of which Uncle Lloyd did not approve was his nephew's occasional absences from home to attend drill with the Porth-madog Volunteers. At this time Lloyd George was on friendly terms with his principal, Randall Casson, and it was clearly Casson who encouraged him to join the Volunteers. He gives an account of one of his experiences on parade in June:

Walked from Llandudno Junction to Camp (at Abergale)—directly I arrived I stripped off my private clothes and put on uniform—got my tea, not at all bad after my tiresome walking. To bed 11. Slept comfortably. Awoke 4.15 a.m. Got up 5.15 and fiddled about until drill-time. I then went without washing to drill and got on quite as well as I expected—it was the 'turns'; I could not very well do them. After drill I pipe-clayed my belt and sling and got some breakfast—stuff which you could not look at in the receptacles it was contained in under ordinary circumstances. Still the meat and butter and bread were very good. Inspection at 9 a.m. At first I had intended to drill with the recruits but somehow by mistake I joined the battalion—(then) a very awkward predicament—my braces broke just before the drill and my trousers were continuously coming down. Mr. Casson noticed it once or twice—the marching but more especially the running in this condition was most awkward—it was very hot and sultry and altogether I felt most miserable and was heartily glad to see the drill over. Arrived at Port. shortly before 11—Singing most of the way—Slept at Mr. Casson's.

On the occasion of another drill he commented: 'The other fellows rather pass me as they attend drills more regularly.'

On other occasions he was sent by Casson to the country to serve writs and other legal documents, and he made the best of these absences on official office business:

1882

Sat. 12 Aug. To Beddgelert with 11 o'clock coach—walking, fearfully hot—had my feet and face blistered—bathed them in Llyn Dinas; serving Writs—Had a glass of port with police officer; had glass of beer before starting from Port with J.B.—another at Prince Llewelyn, Beddgelert and glass of porter with some bread & chop at Thomas' house—so that's keeping the Blue Ribbon Pledge* grandly. Slept at Prince Llewelyn. Very tired.

---

* D.Ll.G had signed the *Blue Ribbon Pledge* (the total abstinence pledge) in 1882. The comment he made in his diary was: 'It may give me somehow an opportunity of exercising, maybe displaying (!) my oratorical (?) powers sometime', an obvious reference to being a platform speaker on behalf of the Temperance movement, an intention which he carried out with effect on many occasions.

Sun. 13 Aug. Paid my bill 2/6 and gave 1/– to waitress. At 11.20 started for Criccieth—Rain stops in 'Pass'—I compose a sort of speech for imaginary Penmachno audience, answering their scoffs at us Xians. At Criccieth (our house) by 3 after stopping at Glaslyn for a glass of beer and at Caerdyni for milk. Then to chapel.

Wed. 16 Aug. Had some beer, bread and cheese in Brynhir Arms—walked to Garn.

Sat. 19 Aug. Reading *Democracy* the popular novel which exposes American politics. My poor studies ! . . Idea struck me that it would not be a bad 'spec' some time to write a novel demonstrating how the poor are neglected in religion and politics, and inculcating a principle of 'religion & politics' for the poor. Bravo.! A really *brave* (Oh!) design.

From his youth Lloyd George inwardly rebelled against the constraints of the Puritanism in which he was brought up by his mother and Uncle Lloyd. He was determined that these constraints should neither dominate nor mould his way of life. Casson was an English lawyer who had settled in Wales mainly to serve the legal needs of the local landed gentry. He was an officer with the Volunteer Corps, and it was as natural for him to drink beer or port as it was for Uncle Lloyd to have a cup of tea. In Casson's view there was nothing wrong in doing some gardening on a Sunday. Occasionally, when Lloyd George spent a week-end with him at Morfa Lodge, he too would lend a hand in some genteel exercise, such as sweeping the front lawn clear of autumn leaves. Casson's influence on his young articled clerk was responsible for Lloyd George's decision, which he tried to keep secret from his mother and uncle, to join the Porthmadog Volunteers and to enjoy a glass of beer with his bread and cheese at a local inn.

He was careful as a rule in not allowing this influence to affect what he did at home. Sometimes, however, he would slip, as the following diary entry reveals:

1884
Sun 29 June Got up 6.15. Planted 'Antonelle' Chrysanthemum, but Mam (Mother) saw me and appeared terribly shocked—so I bolted. . . .

Lloyd George found his Sundays unbearably oppressive as a rule, and Sundays such as the one he mentions above were few and far between. After the stress and memory-testing effort of passing the intermediate examination were over, Uncle Lloyd expected his favourite nephew to play a more prominent role in chapel and to speak on Sundays. Lloyd George was not prepared to do more than read a chapter occasionally in chapel on his home ground at Criccieth, but John Roberts, the Porthmadog Baptist lay-preacher and Republican, who conducted a running tug-of-war with Casson for the young Lloyd George's soul, arranged that he should accompany him on one of his week-end visits to Penmachno, near Betws-y-Coed. The first visit was such a success that others followed, and Lloyd George's diary entries show that these were days when he gained some experience of speaking in chapel, and days also of 'present mirth and present laughter'. In the romantic surroundings of Penmachno he met Miss Jones of Glasgwm. She was probably the first girl with whom he fell in love. After one of the evening services was over, he was seen going for a walk with her along a leafy country lane. She was sweet and twenty. When he returned to the house where John Roberts and he were staying it was already a matter of comment that the good-looking young Baptist preacher had been seen walking out with Miss Jones. Lloyd George commented: 'I am awfully afraid of it becoming known by all the sisterhood and through them to other persons from Porthmadog and Criccieth who may go there to preach.'

John Roberts, a staunch and understanding friend of the young Lloyd George, was not deterred by this rumour-mongering and the occasional week-end evangelical visits to Penmachno continued throughout 1882 and 1883. The affair with Miss Jones petered out —partly on account of some one having told her that 'he was an awful flirt and was having an affair with a Porthmadog girl at the same time', and partly because Lloyd George had written her some letters, which were 'too independent for her liking'. However, Miss Jones told a friend, so Lloyd George recorded: '*Mi ŵyr yr Arglwydd bod well gen i o na neb bûm i efo fo erioed*' (The Lord knows I prefer him to anyone I have ever been with). Soon after Miss Jones broke off her friendship with Lloyd George, she married a local doctor. Lloyd George's comment was:

Well, I am not sorry. . . . I think it is better for her that she should stick to a man who is in a position to give her a comfortable position and not to an unthinking stripling of 19. . . .

The adjective 'unthinking' was an over-harsh self-criticism, as his numerous notes and letters of the Penmachno period testify. Interleaved in his diary for 1882–3 was a note in his father's handwriting, the substance of which Lloyd George transcribed into Welsh for use in his Penmachno addresses. His father's independence of mind and opinion appealed strongly to Lloyd George. This was the note:

Two Articles of New Church Creed
1. The unrestrained love of self, is the root of evil in the human heart.
2. Regeneration consists in the sub-ordination of self-love to the love of God and our neighbour.

During 1882–3, under John Roberts's guidance, Lloyd George regarded himself as a member of a mission whose task was to convert such of the people of Penmachno who cared to listen to a simpler form of the Christian faith than that handed down to them by their fathers. In an exchange of letters, written in Welsh, between Miss Sydney Roberts of Penmachno and Lloyd George in the summer of 1883, Lloyd George made it clear that he was fired by his concern for the souls of others in taking part in the Penmachno mission. Knowing that his views were not entirely orthodox, he showed due regard for the Sabbath, by asking Miss Roberts to hire the use of the small chapel on a week night. Miss Roberts wrote him that she could not give him a definite answer:

Henrhiw Uchaf,
Penmachno.

I can tell you for sure that the people of Penmachno like the people of Porthmadog and Criccieth are exceedingly content with their religious arrangements and they know what we are standing for. For goodness sake, just you think of the two sons of my uncle John Williams. From a religious standpoint they are as enthusiastic as anyone and regard the order of the Methodists and Wesleyans as correct, and they are convinced that, if they comply with their ordinances, they will be saved.

To tell you the truth, I have felt very troubled ever since I received your letter—and I don't like the thought of you regarding me as unenthusiastic.

Your sister in the faith,
SYDNEY ROBERTS

Lloyd George made a carbon copy of his hand-written reply, in Welsh:

As one of many of us, who have taken an oath before heaven and earth, to be a good soldier of Him, who died for us, I could not rest from doing my part without betraying my trust. . . . I cannot believe that you really mean what your letter certainly conveys—namely, that the attempt to spread the words which bring eternal life amongst your neighbours have pained you—made you *very troubled.* . . .

It is selfish and unworthy of a kind man to be content to inherit life eternal for himself, while allowing others he knows to drown in death.
[My italics.]

This statement of his position as a Christian is consistent with his declared principal ambition in life—to promote himself by benefiting others. A later passage in this letter indicated that he was not a man to be put off from pursuing his objective:

Now I am certain of this; whatever contempt was expressed concerning anything which was said, no one had more scorn poured on him than I. I had been *one only* amongst all the young men of my profession—as you know it's a profession which is not noted for its piety. But I believe—rather I hope—I would feel happy, not miserable, when I'm subjected to contempt because I'm given an opportunity to do some small work for Jesus who has done so much for me. This is no boast—I would be ashamed to boast about so small a contribution as mine; especially so, after reading about the saints, whose history has been recorded to instruct and inspire us,—those of us who are happy to be considered worthy of suffering scorn for his Name's sake. . . .

> I am, your brother in the faith,
> D. Lloyd George.

In a Welsh essay Lloyd George wrote on *Amcan Bywyd* (The Purpose of Life) for the Christmas 1882 meeting of the Porthmadog Debating Society, he adopted several of his father's views and thoughts as recorded in the latter's notebooks. He declared that the main purpose of man's life on earth was to glorify his creator and went on to ask:

And how is he to reflect his Father's glory? By going about doing good, by diminishing man's misery in every respect and by promoting his happiness. In this respect Jesus Christ is the *great model*. He consecrated his life on earth to do the will of his Father in heaven.

An impression has gained ground recently that Lloyd George's temperament was not, in fact, religious and that he lacked the transcendental sense.* The truth is that Lloyd George, like many people, held and expressed opinions which sometimes appeared contradictory. He was frank enough to record these contradictory views and to tell his brother and one or two close friends, such as D. R. Daniel, of his religious doubts and difficulties. For example on Saturday, 21 April 1883, he wrote in his diary:

Per 6.10 p.m. train to Port. Attended company drill—They believe at home that I have gone to listen to 'Y Diwygiwr' [revivalist], but I

---

* This is the view expressed by John Grigg in *The Young Lloyd George*, Eyre Methuen, 1973, pp. 33–5.

thought that I would get more *'gwynfyd'* [blessedness] physically & mentally by getting a good exercise, drilling & skirmishing—there until 7.45—so I lost tail-end of Revivalist's sermon, which I had intended particularly to hear. Moreover, I missed a treat—there was *'gorfoledd'* [ecstasy] there to-night.

This particular revivalist visited Criccieth the following day, but Richard Lloyd was not impressed by the religious emotion generated by evangelical fervour of this kind. In reference to the visit Richard Lloyd recorded in his diary:

1882

Sun. 22 April More people here to-day than I've ever seen on a Sunday. All chapels closed, it seems, except ours after the morning.

23 May Criccieth Fair. Many young people openly cuddling and wandering about like summer ducks. O that the Revival did not spread from the chapel to the Fair! There would be some point to it then.

In emphasizing the importance of religious faith having practical results Lloyd George was at one with his Uncle Lloyd. An entry Lloyd George made in his diary in February 1883, shows how aware he then was of the power over him of transcendental influences, be they of the Devil or of God.

The occasion for the entry was a late-night visit he made to Porthmadog against his better judgement:

Just fancy, I would not have believed it myself, if some one were to have told me a twelve month ago. I am dangerously easy to be led. The Devil must lose a deal—an immensity of his cunning if he does not easily persuade me to be a member of his pandemonial society. But No! Thanks to Omnipotent Love, who is far more winsome & attractive, he may yet lead me.

In this essay, *Amcan Bywyd*, he expressly rejected atheism. He accepted the reality of God and the validity of the Christian faith:

Then again there's Atheism; this is a mistaken attitude concerning the true purpose of life, and what lies at the root of this misconception is the incorrect belief that life consists only of our short-lived existence in this world. . . . By challenging his Creator, when he is young, a man does not perhaps suffer any pangs of conscience; but when he grows older, he starts to suffer from the damage he has done to his spirit. He has deeply wounded his spiritual personality and the signs of ill-health manifest themselves.

If you want to know who attains real happiness—whether the

109

atheist who lives to deny his God, or the Christian who lives to praise him, compare the condition of Voltaire, the arch-Atheist, and the condition of Paul, the supreme hero of the Faith. . . . Voltaire made a leap into the outer darkness, whilst Paul knew that death opened up the dark places for him to enter into the inheritance of the saints in the light. . . . The greatest glory the great Creator of the Universe can receive from man is for man to grow to maturity in beauty of mind and body. That is why gluttony, drunkenness and excessive dissipation are such despicable sins—they detract from the glory of God by defiling man.

D.Ll.G

Nevertheless he continued to find chapel services, with the abiding exception of listening to Uncle Lloyd's sermons, boring in the extreme. The following are typical references to the subject, both in the year 1884:

Sun. 2 March Believe in my heart of hearts—and I told my brother William to-day—that a good walk on such a beautiful day would have shown far greater appreciation of the Blessing than sticking in a musty hovel to listen to the mumbling of musty prayers and practice.

Sun. 12 October Got up 7. Fine morning—Took a walk as far as Dwyfor. Nothing convinced me more than this walk of the scandalous waste of opportunities involved in a chapel—huddling a religion of pseudos—the calm and beauty of the scenery breathed far more divinity than all the psalmodies and prayers of a million congregated churches.

Richard Crossman, reviewing *The Young Lloyd George*,* remarked that Lloyd George's decision to support the Boer cause in the South African War was the first occasion in his political life when he seemed to have been actuated not by ambition but by moral indignation and that to this day no one knows why he did so. It is unfortunate that the impression has been created that the spiritual luggage carried by Lloyd George was light and of little account. Moral and religious questions exercised his mind to an extent surprising in a young solicitor in his early twenties. His decision to preach in Penmachno, regardless of the attitude of more orthodox Christians, had shown to those who knew him then that he was prepared to follow a course which he considered morally right.

He declared in January 1884 that he accepted the views of the

---

* In *The Listener*, 21 June 1973; John Grigg, Eyre Methuen.

Positivist Society on the regeneration of humanity, but he believed that this 'grand truth is taught in a far grander way—and in a way which appeals more powerfully to man's heart—by Christianity.' 'This', he added, 'is Christianity and Christianity is this; and I mean to teach so one day.'

A reference Lloyd George made in 1884 to Bradlaugh underlines his total lack of sympathy with the atheist's standpoint. As if the Irish problem, the schism between Gladstone and Chamberlain, the troubles in Egypt and the Sudan were not enough, Gladstone's administration during 1880–5 was marred by Bradlaugh's initial refusal to take the oath of allegiance to enable him to take his seat in Parliament. Bradlaugh was not prepared to swear allegiance in the name of a God, whose existence he denied. Gladstone wished to have passed the Religious Disabilities Bill enabling Bradlaugh and others like-minded to affirm rather than swear their allegiance. He was unable to muster a sufficient majority and the Bill remained a dead letter, when Bradlaugh was re-elected in the 1884 election. Lloyd George commented: 'I almost wish he hadn't [been]. I had never much faith in him as a champion of liberty.'

When Lloyd George passed this uncharitable and probably impetuous judgement on Bradlaugh, he revealed a chink in his political armour which was to cost him dearly in later years. Bradlaugh, whether his contemporaries agreed with his refusal to take the oath or not, was taking his stand on a point of principle, and his persistence led eventually to Parliament passing the Religious Disabilities Removal Act in 1891, by which time Bradlaugh was dying and was unconscious of what had been done. Lloyd George was, in fact, recording as his own personal opinion of Bradlaugh the view generally held by the majority of nonconformists. It was the combined vote of the Catholics and nonconformists which had kept the Bill off the statute book for ten years. After Bradlaugh's death Gladstone commented:

A distinguished man and an admirable member of this House, was laid yesterday in his mother-earth. He was the subject of a long controversy in this house . . . but does anybody who hears me believe that that controversy, so prosecuted and so abandoned, was beneficial to the Christian religion?

Lloyd George was fully aware of the importance of strongly held nonconformist opinions on issues of the day in the Wales of the 1880s and 1890s. As a member of a numerically tiny religious sect he could not rely on the support of the strong Calvinistic Methodist connexion unless he could adopt and advocate their ideas of what constituted the good society. He was ambitious to make a noteworthy career for himself, to excel in life and to have his talent and success in benefiting others through his efforts generally recognized. So far as the landed gentry and the Anglican Church were concerned, he was a complete outsider. To achieve success it was essential for him to win the nonconformist vote. He soon realized that one of the most effective ways of winning a good name for himself with them was to be an effective advocate for the Temperance cause. He was really running an appalling political risk in frequenting pubs, particularly on a Sunday! I believe he must have been frightened by his audacity in visiting local inns for the occasional drink during the summer of 1882 and, so far as the records go, he appears to have dropped the practice. His taste for alcohol never developed from this modest beginning in the hot summer days of 1882 and he had probably taken a tight hold on his Blue Ribbon pledge of total abstinence once more when he addressed a Temperance meeting in Llanystumdwy in December 1882. After some initial nervousness and 'stammerings & stutterings' on his part he recorded that the speech was well received. The chairman said he had made some reference to passing an Act of Parliament to squelch the evil and added that he expected Lloyd George would soon be in Parliament himself to pass such measures. Mary Ellen, Lloyd George's sister, was present at the meeting and gave a glowing account of the good impression the speech had created in Llanystumdwy. Uncle Lloyd was mightily pleased.

Lloyd George spoke at many Temperance meetings after this, and indeed first made his reputation as a public speaker on the Temperance issue. He was due to sit his final examination in January 1884 so that he could become a qualified solicitor within days of attaining his twenty-first birthday. But because of the variety of interests other than the law which occupied his mind and time during 1883 particularly, it is not surprising that he did not sit his final examination until April 1884. The 1880s constituted a period of depression in both trade and industry. The appeal to husbands and fathers to abstain from spending their meagre wages on drink was a strong one both on social and moral grounds. Lloyd George's mind was often occupied with thoughts of the impoverished condition of such down-trodden members of society, as tenant-farmers or industrial workers. This interest led him to read the books of Henry George, the American political economist, when he should have been studying his textbooks. Henry George was a great egalitarian, advocating the equal right of all men to the use of the earth. He believed that the private ownership of land could not be justified, and compared the soil to the air or sunlight, over which no man claimed ownership. Man's right to the private ownership of things manufactured by him was recognized by Henry George as absolute.

At one time Lloyd George's interest in Henry George's book *Progress and Poverty* was such that he bought it with money he should have spent on his subscription to the Law Lending Library, with the result that he could not afford to borrow the next textbook he needed for his legal studies. Some months after buying this book, and after reading the account of a lecture Henry George had given at St. George's Hall, Liverpool, Lloyd George recorded in his diary the following opinion he had formed on Henry George's main thesis:

1884

11 January I don't believe in his scheme—Appropriation of the rent is nothing but aimless plunder. The great object is to get control of the *land itself* into the hands of those whose interests are so vitally affected by it—And it strikes me that almost every argument applicable to such confiscation is also an argument for State appropriation of personal property. My own idea is the devolution to the State of deceased owners' properties, so that all alike may have an equal chance of starting life.

The reading of Henry George's books was not the cause of Lloyd George's profound interest in the land as a political issue, although it stimulated his radical thoughts on the topic during his formative years. In November 1882 he recorded:

Finished reading A. M. Sullivan's *New Ireland*. It gives the Irish Question in a new light—of course, it is partial to Irishmen, but I think that on the whole he is about fair. It has had one effect on me— it has made me more Irish than before even.

He had already noted that Michael Davitt was his 'most admired character in real life', and that, with Gladstone and Chamberlain, Parnell was held in high regard by him. The Irish national revival in the 1880s was led by Davitt and Parnell; Davitt, as leader of the Land League, encouraged threatened tenant farmers to resort to unconstitutional means against their eviction, whilst Parnell, as leader of the Irish party in the Westminster Parliament, sought a constitutional solution to the Irish question by the passing of a Home Rule Bill. Parnell accepted Davitt's invitation to become President of the Land League, so as to make it plain to all and sundry that there was no real division between the two leaders of Irish opinion. The Land League was declared illegal in 1881 and both Davitt and Parnell were imprisoned. They were released from prison on Gladstone's initiative in April 1882. In pursuance of his policy of conciliation Gladstone appointed two new ministers to represent the English Government in Dublin Castle. Both were assassinated in Phoenix Park in May 1882 shortly after their appointment. Parnell publicly condemned the murders, but rumour had it that he had in fact condoned the murders by the 'Invincible Assassins'. W. E. Forster, who had resigned from office because Gladstone had refused to renew the Coercion Act, was a bitter enemy of Parnell and accused him publicly of having foreknowledge of them. He made this allegation in April 1883, and this stimulated Lloyd George to make the following outspoken comment on the Irish question in his diary:

1883

24 April Read Forster's terrible charges against Parnell—Also read Parnell's reply. As a fact I do not believe that Parnell had any knowledge of the 'Invincible Assassins'—But I do firmly believe that he in a way connived at or rather palliated murder in some instances—and rightly so, as I believe; the murder of such wretches as Lord Limerick for instance was an act of political justice and expediency of the highest order; as an act of justice it was neither more or less than meting out due punishment to a murderer of the blackest dye (that is an evicting landlord), who would otherwise escape punishment; as an act of political expediency it seemed to call attention to the corrupt and atrocious social system, which permitted and condoned murder by the landlord and justified the tenant assassinations. That is my candid opinion. But it would not do for Parnell publicly to admit this— It would bring him within the power of the law—and most important of all, it might be construed by both fanatics and villains as a justification and incitement for all murder.

The above statement of his close bond of sympathy with the cause of the Irish rebel and out-and-out Nationalist is, in my view, impossible to reconcile with comments he made on Gladstone's Egyptian policy, particularly with reference to the Sudan. Whilst the Irish question is still very much with us, the Egypt of the 1880s has little interest for us today. On 11 July 1884, the British fleet, on the instructions of Gladstone's administration, unilaterally bombarded Alexandria, the French fleet having withdrawn and the French government having previously informed the British government that the proposed operation would be an act of war against Egypt. Bright resigned from the government in protest. Lloyd George commented that he did not understand 'this Egyptian question', but the young Imperialist within him proclaimed: 'I am rather glad of the splendid practice of our guns.' He declared he was depressed at the news of the reverses suffered by the army in the course of the Sudan campaign and criticized Gladstone, influenced apparently by the Marquis of Salisbury's speeches in the House of Lords. Lloyd George was characterized from the dawning of his political awareness by a dichotomy of outlook; within the young Irish and Welsh nationalist rebel, there lurked the young Imperialist, who warmed to the sound of the British Army marching overseas. His roots were firmly planted in the soil of Llanystumdwy, but from an early age two branches growing in opposing directions sprang from the trunk. Many Welshmen consider that Lloyd George started out as a politician whose interest was confined to Welsh issues during the 1880s and 1890s and that the South African war widened his political outlook: but in fact the wider interest was there from a much earlier date.

At the beginning of 1884, shortly before he went to sit his final examination, he wrote:

I am more inclined for a London career—a fellow may make a successful lawyer down here and amass a tidy—tho not a large fortune; but as for any higher object—fame—London is the place for that. If I were to pursue my great ambition—to be eminent as a public speaker—in Wales that would be almost an impossibility. For one thing, there are so many good, excellent speakers already—Another thing—I would have to speak in Welsh, so that my reputation would after all be confined to this stinted principality. À la Londres.

The intention Lloyd George formed at the beginning of 1884 to live in London may well have been precipitated by an unhappy love affair. When entrusting his diaries to my father he had told him that some of the most important entries were in shorthand, and his references to this affair are mainly in shorthand. The girl with whom he fell in love was a well-known local singer, Liza Jones, who frequently was unable to keep her appointments with him on account of her singing engagements in Caernarfonshire and Merionethshire. He recorded the details of where they should have met and her detailed explanation for failing to meet him.

1883
2 Dec. What anguish it would have saved me if I had known it in time [i.e. her explanation]. Let every young man beware in time of falling in love. It is replete with peril.

Sun. 25 Nov. A miserable Sunday in all respects for me. . . . My feet wet all day owing to leaky shoes, but [shorthand] above everything. L. went to Beddgelert on Friday to sing in an Entertainment there and in spite of my earnest request that she would not go, but the

little Jezebel has stayed there over Sunday, which has given me un-
utterable pain throughout the day. In earnest I do not know what to
do with the girl. I wish to God I had never meddled with her, but I
am afraid it is too late now. She has acquired a wonderful mastery over
my idiot-heart.

A young schoolmaster in a neighbouring village, who later became known throughout Wales as an authority on Welsh folk-
songs, had in fact also fallen in love with the young singer. Liza
must have realized that she had more in common with Lloyd
Williams, the school-master, than she had with Lloyd George, and
she became Mrs. Lloyd Williams. There was no rancour or ill-
feeling and Lloyd Williams, who eventually became Professor of
Botany at the University of Wales, remained on friendly terms
with Lloyd George throughout his life.

The reference to 'leaky shoes' in the above diary entry is revealing. The family were living under almost intolerable conditions
of respectable poverty in Criccieth at this period. Richard Lloyd's
diary contains many instances of the effect of this poverty on the
family:

1883
5 June My dear children, I would like to see them established with
some business on hand. . . . I feel dreadfully that I have borrowed as
I have when they eat their mid-day meal. I remember with affection
the school-years in the old home—and the families with whom I was
familiar.

23 June Find my name is down as a subscriber for a book of English
sermons—4/-. The thought that my limited means do not enable me
to spend 4/- on a book stabs me with a pang.

10 July Two strangers called to-day, took lodgings—we paid back
to-day the £2 Betsy [Elizabeth George] had borrowed from W.W.
[William Williams was Richard Lloyd's fellow unpaid pastor of Berea
Chapel at Criccieth. He was a Criccieth draper, whose generosity,
coupled with two or three others, enabled the family to pull through
during the Criccieth years, before the legal practice was established by
the two brothers.]

24 Nov. Recd. £1 from W.W. loan to be paid back—to pay D.Ll.G's
Law Library Subscription.
1884
9 Jan. Called at Ynysgain—Uncle still pretty poorly. He lent me
£2/10/- for my sister Betsy to buy flour.

4 Feb. Recd 10/- from W.W. to-day towards the needs of our family—

felt it keenly lest it might inconvenience him. I'll have to turn to & eat what there is of honey left in the hive before it completely vanishes. [This was a reference to the remaining building society funds left by William George senior.]

23 Feb. William's birthday. I regret I have nothing better to give him than my good wishes.

12 April Rec. £1 of W.W. to pay for slippers etc. for D.Ll. G.

To add to the family's difficulties at this period Lloyd George was struck down at least twice with very severe bouts of quinsy, to which he was prone. My father remembered him having one of these attacks when they were boys sleeping together in the wainscot bed at Highgate. He appeared to be on the verge of suffocation when Uncle Lloyd and his mother managed to get a goose-quill dipped in honey down his throat. My father was always convinced that this saved his brother's life. When he had these attacks at Criccieth Uncle Lloyd used to sleep with him and remain awake for nights on end so that he could help him to recover his breath whenever Lloyd George awoke with a fright, unable to breathe. During March and April 1884 before leaving for London to sit his final examination Lloyd George made a superhuman effort to catch up with his legal studies and time lost by illness and other interests. He regularly stayed up studying till the early hours of the morning, snatching only four or five hours sleep before getting down to his textbooks again. He told Uncle Lloyd that he could not possibly manage to sit the honours examination. Uncle Lloyd was dreadfully disappointed, and just before he left for London Uncle Lloyd said that Lloyd George fell into a fit of low mood. He tried, apparently without success, every possible thing to get him out of it. Lloyd George was worn out when he arrived in London, felt very ill and on the night before the examination recorded in his diary: 'Bad headache and neuralgia. To bed 11.30, weary and ill—almost crying.' He said that he nearly fainted in Holborn as he made his way to the Law Society's Hall in Chancery Lane. However on arrival there he was cheered by an encouraging letter from Uncle Lloyd and 'a most comic letter' from William, which made him laugh. He stayed with a cousin, a member of the Ynysgain family, whom Uncle Lloyd records as having helped them out on several occasions during this moneyless period.

As he sat the examination he gained confidence and believed that he had answered the questions sufficiently well to pass. He decided after all to sit the honours examination and stayed on as his cousin's guest in London for a week. He appears to have spent most of his free time sermon-tasting and visiting the House of Commons. He considered that English preachers lacked 'that impassioned, appealing oratory which characterizes Welsh preaching'. He added: 'Spurgeon, however, is a capital speaker I must say he was very inspiring—he almost galvanized my dead faith into something like a transient somnolence, if not life.' In the House of Commons on Monday, 28 April he heard 'The Grand Old Man. He is really grand—there is no one so outstanding. His voice is indescribable, rather husky at first, but when it clears up it is piercing and silvery. His manner is rather vehement. The way he dressed Raikes brought the House and Gallery down. The scorn and bitterness of his voice was inimitable.'

News that he had passed reached Criccieth on 11 May and on 27 May he heard that he had obtained Third Class Honours. Lloyd George commented:

All quite delighted—especially my fond old Uncle, who had only last night assured me that he did not concern himself about Honours in the least; but I knew by his countenance that he did. What troubled me most was that I knew my failure would disappoint him so much.

Richard Lloyd was also pleased that William was progressing so well with his articles. He had happened to meet Randall Casson one day and had been given the best possible opinion of the boys. He noted in his diary that Casson went on: 'My partner and I have been discussing William. Our joint opinion is that we have never encountered the equal of William and his brother. He is steady with his work and understands what he is about.' They sent William to Caernarfon on some office business of importance. Uncle Lloyd commented:

Although I would rather have seen D.Ll.G being asked, yet pleased that Wil Bach so business-like in the matter.

It was soon to become apparent how fortunate the family were and Lloyd George, in particular, that brother William was so steady in his work and understood what he was about.

CHAPTER SEVEN

MARRIAGE AND PARTNERSHIP

In his poem, 'Parnell', Yeats wrote:*

Parnell came down the road, he said to a cheering man:
'Ireland shall get her freedom and you still break stone.'

Lloyd George had hoped that by passing his final examination and qualifying as a solicitor he would have gained his freedom and obtained a legal appointment of some sort in London. Nevertheless in the stony days of the 1880s the only opening he could find was to return to work with Breese, Jones & Casson as an assistant solicitor until something better turned up. Randall Casson told him that he could not offer him more than a nominal salary as the firm's actual receipts fell far short of their earnings. Ordinary folk just did not have the money to pay solicitors' bills in those days, and Legal Aid was unheard of. He offered Lloyd George one pound a week, at the same time saying that he did not suggest that this was any indication of the newly qualified solicitor's worth. Lloyd George agreed to accept the offer, provided he received a commission on each transaction introduced by him, and Casson assented to this. Neither of them realized at the time what bitterness this provision for commission was to cause between them.

The family's financial resources were so exiguous following Lloyd George's acceptance of this offer that he could not raise the £3 required to buy the season railway ticket between Criccieth and Porthmadog. Both Richard Lloyd and Lloyd George were apparently too proud to admit themselves that the young solicitor, who was joining his old firm in Porthmadog, could not lay his hands on this £3 which was urgently required, and in the end William agreed to obtain a loan for the purpose from cousin John of Caerdyni, Criccieth. Lloyd George then took up his appointment on 12 May 1884 and within a fortnight William was recording in his diary.†

---

* *Last Poems* (1936–1939) in *Collected Poems*, Macmillan, 1952, p. 359.
† All William George's diary entries have been transcribed from shorthand.

Skirmish between David and Mr. Casson. They are both too sensitive to live long in peace together. David uneasy about his future.

To supplement his tiny income Lloyd George borrowed some money from Thomas Jones, another Porthmadog solicitor, which he took care to repay as and when he could by instalments of £2. During July 1884 the rent was in arrear on the Criccieth house, but Lloyd George objected strongly to his mother and Richard Lloyd taking in visitors. Richard Lloyd recorded the occasion:

1884
4 July Lady called to see the house—wants a bedroom and sitting-room. We offered her accommodation for 25/-, but she says she won't take them, because D.Ll.G says, if she comes, he'll go away! What can we do in the face of this situation now? I called at Ynysgain, but Uncle hasn't anything to lend for the time being.

A few days later Lloyd George appears to have changed his mind, and William recorded that they were 'cleaning the place for lodgers', adding satirically, 'David having given his gracious consent'. The family's circumstances were so bad at one time that summer that Richard Lloyd had to turn to his fellow deacon William Williams for the loan of £3 towards paying the bill of £4 for the supply of farm butter. Mary Ellen George was without 4s to pay the return fare to Caernarfon for the day to attend an Eisteddfod and Lloyd George says he managed to find 4s to give her.

During these summer and autumn months the situation between Casson and Lloyd George deteriorated to such an extent that they were not on speaking terms, and William found himself in the invidious position of being asked by Lloyd George to deliver written notes to Casson. Casson was very annoyed at this turn of events. In all this Lloyd George was much more concerned with his own injured feelings and with his antagonism towards Casson than with the possible effects of these rows on his brother's relationship with the firm. There were ups and downs in the continuing battle between them. William became obviously upset, and it was Casson who took the initiative shortly before Christmas 1884 in making things easier for him. He told him to stay at home and give himself up entirely to study for a short time, and after the examination was over to stay on in London for a week or so. He offered to pay for William's lodgings if he were unable to stay with his London cousin.

Whilst William was away in London during January 1885 sitting his intermediate law examination, which he passed, Casson agreed
120

to release Lloyd George to enable him to start in practice on his own hook. William returned to resume his work as articled clerk to find that Lloyd George had set up in practice in opposition to the firm. William's reaction was:

Now that David is in opposition I am afraid I shall have many delicate and difficult passes to go through. They will be afraid to entrust me with confidential matters, in case I might at some future date use that knowledge against them.

Lloyd George was, of course, unable to engage a solicitor's clerk to help him, but within a fortnight of his brother's return from London he started to give him clerical work to do out of office hours. William George commented: 'David gave me a job which lasted till 2 a.m. Another development of his character.' My father could, of course, have refused, but the family desperately needed the money. Naturally, Casson was annoyed that William was helping Lloyd George, and during February he made things unpleasant for William. Richard Lloyd commented:

1885
27 Feb. Sorry to hear that Casson is fulfilling his threat to make things unpleasant for Wm. on account of his brother. . . . Will not have this, to ill-treat Wm. to indulge their furious annoyance with his brother.

William found that one week he was made to feel a complete outsider in his principal's office, being 'almost frowned out of existence', whereas the next week he was allowed to bask in the sunshine of their smiles and favours. He added:

Fickle folk. I will try to take advantage of both moods. The first to test and husband my self-confidence. The second to impress upon them the signs of my youthful intelligence, to show that I may be of some advantage or disadvantage to them just as they make use of me. . . .
The dark shadow of David's inability to carry on on his own account haunted me all day. It is lamentable. David is full of big things. He is going to retire, to go in for reporting. . . . He is going to revenge [himself on Casson].

Lloyd George kept a detailed diary of his legal and other activities throughout 1885, his first year of practising on his own as a solicitor. Bearing in mind the poverty with which the family were afflicted, the indifferent health of his uncle and widowed mother, the strain on William both of preparing himself without any tuition to sit his final examination and remaining loyal to the solicitors with whom he was articled in spite of his brother's onslaughts on Casson, what strikes me in these diary entries is Lloyd George's almost total absorption with his own personal dream to succeed and to have his talent, success and superiority recognized by others. William George was once ticked off by him that summer because he did not enthuse over some triumph Lloyd George thought he had scored up, either in court or in the Debating Society—the record does not make clear the occasion. William's diary comment is, however, significant in that it shows he appreciated Lloyd George's need, which he never lost, for flattery and praise even for things said or done in the daily course of events, things which are generally taken for granted, particularly within the family. William himself had taken more after his father than David and had inherited something of his father's oversensitivity to criticism. Both these facets of the brother's characters are evident in William's diary entry:

How was it that I went so clumsy with David? I must really try not to look cold or indifferent. The look is greater than the intention. Still it will militate against me unless I strive against it. As Uncle said in his sermon sometime ago—Paul could *praise* as well as blame as he saw occasion. . . . David is sensitive. David certainly is offended.

David's health was also a worry to his family. William gives an account of the Sunday in January 1884 when Lloyd George's studies were seriously interrupted by the attack of quinsy which according to Richard Lloyd nearly killed him:

Uncle told me on Sunday that he was in danger. An indescribable Sunday and a more indescribable Sunday night. . . . The terrors of death. I think I would prefer to be ill myself in future than for David to be ill. For two reasons: (1) I could not undergo greater horrors. I would in fact be more composed and (2) I could make those round me more comfortable than they are with David. He is so peevish!

Lloyd George had another sore throat in October 1885, and he records the occasion as follows:

Another very bad throat. M.E.G. up with me all night. Dr. called twice. (Mam sat up with me.) Dr. said I was very weak and that I should get some stimulant. Got bottle of Port from Bowens—Just as I had gone to bed, swelling burst and considerable amount of matter exuded. Was to have addressed Temperance meeting in Pwllheli tonight. Feel happy somehow to-day. It was only to-day I fully realized the object of pain in the design of Creation—Happiness cannot be fully enjoyed without occasional misery.

But throughout 1884 and 1885 the struggle to keep going materially was inevitably uppermost in Lloyd George's mind. It is characteristic that he never lost sight of his overriding ambition to become a public speaker who would surpass his contemporaries by the force of his eloquence and cogency of his arguments. Each court case was judged not so much on its legal or factual merits, but in the light of the opportunity it provided for him to test and improve his style of speech. In February 1885, when according to Richard Lloyd, Casson was making things unpleasant for William, Lloyd George was having his first experience of conducting court cases of his own. In Lloyd George's detailed accounts of some of these minor cases I have failed to find any reference to his brother's predicament, caught as he was between two fires. On 25 February 1885 Lloyd George recorded that he lost most of the cases he had that day in Porthmadog County Court, the judge being dead against him, and that Mr. Casson 'did his worst' towards him in all these cases; nevertheless he won one case, and commented:

I was prouder of having won this than annoyed at having lost the others. What I was most astounded and elated at in the whole course of to-day's proceedings was the fluency and expressiveness of speech I displayed. Hitherto I had been a miserable failure in this respect, but to-day I commanded quite an interminable torrent of words and the Judge rather complained of my long speeches, i.e. in his own $\frac{1}{2}$ blunt, $\frac{1}{2}$ good-natured way. . . . The Judge said—'I am afraid Mr. George if you are in this case it will take some time.' I should have been astonished if anyone had told me in the morning that before the evening sun had set I should have gained a reputation for having too much to say in Court. I believe Mr. Casson's nasty, mean conduct was the greatest impetus to my eloquence; it nerved and aroused my utmost spirit and power. Then to Chapel. Walking about the W.J. Feel very fagged and worried.

When he got home that evening Lloyd George told the family that Casson was now a 'deadly enemy'. Richard Lloyd's abiding conviction in his adopted nephew's near-infallibility was momentarily shaken. If David carried out his threat to revenge himself on Casson, Richard Lloyd was worried as to the adverse effect this would have on William. He also thought that to talk of revenge in this context was unchristian and told David so in no uncertain terms, but added: 'No harm will come of it so long as you will guard yourself against the temptation to retaliate.'

An indication of the general poverty of the 1880s is that one of Lloyd George's earliest instructions was to act for the Official Receiver in the collection of small debts due to the estate of a bankrupt village shopkeeper. He enlisted the help of Richard Lloyd to help him out with the humdrum clerical work. Richard Lloyd commented: 'Very difficult job. Do not think D. will gain anything with this job; very poor lot. Some of the best have already been collected.' What prompted this comment was the knowledge that the only remuneration his nephew would receive would be the commission on the sums collected from the bankrupt's debtors.

The financial mainstay of any country solicitors' practice has always been the preparation of deeds relating to freehold and leasehold properties. Lloyd George was well aware of this, but the general lack of available capital made such instructions few and far between. I once asked my father to sum up his recollection of the early days in practice, and he aptly replied: 'Faith without Deeds.' It is a measure of Lloyd George's greatness that in periods of adversity his will to succeed never deserted him and that he did not despise 'the day of small things'.

When he received instructions in his first poaching case the evidence was heavily loaded against him, but he learnt by heart alternative speeches for the defence and recited them to his brother whilst walking along the path leading from Criccieth to the estuary of the Dwyfor. In court he decided which of the two addresses he would use. In his 1885 diary he referred to the matter as 'this all-important case'. He recorded the reception his address to the Bench had with evident satisfaction. His client was only fined £1. The Chairman's remark particularly pleased him:

'We have no doubt about the case notwithstanding *the very able speech* of Mr. George.' I was very much complimented by everyone in my face and in my absence as well I am told.

He gained most of his experience in public speaking at this period as a member of the Criccieth Debating Society. He gave as much detailed attention to the preparation and delivery of his addresses to this society as he gave in later years to important political speeches before the House of Commons or on the public platform. The society elected him their chairman and he assumed office as if he were accepting an appointment to one of the most important posts in the kingdom. The matters selected for debate covered a wide range of topics, such as the reform of the licensing laws by the introduction of local option, free trade and the disestablishment of the Church in Wales. He first gained his laurels as a public speaker in Criccieth by a speech he made on this latter issue. He recorded a lengthy account of his speech and of the debate in his diary in March 1885. He concluded his entry, obviously elated by his success:

My story about '*rhoi pen yr ysbeiliwr ar ysgwydd y porthmon*' [placing a robber's head on the drover's shoulders] excited peals of laughter,— and when I laid claim to the church's endowments on the ground of Wm. Salisbury, a lawyer, being the first translator of the Bible, I thought I couldn't get on owing to the laughter it raised. *When I sat down I felt I had made my mark in Criccieth.* I saw sensible men, of good position, shaking with laughter whilst I was at it. Not one of the previous or subsequent speeches evoked such a thorough, profound response from the audience both non-conformist and churchman. . . . Liberal Committee after the meeting. I was appointed one of the delegates to Caernarfon. Uncle (who had undoubtedly kept away from meeting for fear of showing too much excitement on my behalf) mightily pleased at my success. A.J.P. said my speech was by far the best, very eloquent. . . .

As the spring and summer of 1885 progressed Lloyd George found himself being drawn closer and closer to the vortex of political activity, which was destined within a few years to engulf him. Richard Lloyd became increasingly concerned:

1885
30 April D.Ll.G off to Ffestiniog for week-end. A.T. exceedingly disappointed he had not prepared Notice as promised. Great pity. Should leave all things to attend to business.

At Blaenau Ffestiniog Lloyd George stayed with Dr. Evans,* one of the earliest of active Lloyd George supporters who did everything possible to help him, both politically and by giving him some of his earliest instructions. Indeed, largely owing to Dr. Evans's help, Lloyd George opened a small one-room office in a terrace house at Blaenau Ffestiniog, to which he travelled by the narrow-gauge railway from Porthmadog on the quarryman's train every Saturday. His association with Blaenau Ffestiniog and Dr. Evans brought him into contact with the active radical movement in Merioneth, a movement which concentrated mainly on the land issue. In February 1886 he met Michael Davitt at Dr. Evans's house, after speaking on the same platform and this turned out to be an exceedingly important meeting in Lloyd George's early political career.

Meanwhile the Criccieth Debating Society reflected the general political mood of the 1885 period by discussing the Franchise and Redistribution Acts of that year, and incidentally passing at one of

---

* Dr. Evans's son, Thomas Carey-Evans, married David Lloyd George's daughter Olwen—now Lady Olwen Carey-Evans, D.B.E.

their meetings a resolution in favour of giving women the vote. Lloyd George himself was very critical of Gladstone's decision to parley with the Marquis of Salisbury, the leader of the Tory party, on this issue. The success of Gladstone and Salisbury in reforming the electoral system by a confidential exchange of views was a prelude to private conferences which led to a coalition between the Irish nationalists under Parnell and the Tories. Gladstone's concern with Irish policies had been consistent throughout most of his parliamentary career. In 1845 he had declared: 'Ireland! Ireland! That cloud in the West—that coming storm!' Many leading Welsh radicals of the 1880s considered that he had been so obsessed with Ireland that he had utterly failed to apply to Wales reforms in relation to oppressive land laws and the disestablishment of the Church, which he had already granted to Ireland. Their doubts concerning Gladstone's Welsh policy were strengthened by Joseph Chamberlain, as the rift between Gladstone and the Liberal-Unionists widened during 1885–6. When Gladstone was promoting his Home Rule for Ireland Bill, Chamberlain declared in a letter to *The Baptist*:

Is it possible that the Nonconformists of Wales are prepared to accept such a situation? They have apparently supported, without much examination, the Irish bills of Mr. Gladstone, under the impression that, by doing so, they will arrive more quickly at the realization of their own hopes.

In June 1885 Gladstone's divided and weakened Liberal government was defeated by twelve votes over the Budget. Gladstone resigned and was replaced by Lord Salisbury's minority Conservative government. This did not last long and a General Election was held in November 1885. Parnell advised Irishmen to vote Tory and similar advice was given by the Catholic bishops in England. The election resulted in the Liberals having 335 seats, the Tories 249 seats and the Irish nationalists 86 seats. The latter under Parnell's leadership accordingly held the balance of power. A Tory minority government, depending on Irish nationalist support, was again formed, but only lasted until January 1886, when it was defeated and Gladstone invited to form another Liberal government under his premiership, an invitation which he accepted with some misgiving. In April 1886, Gladstone introduced a Bill for Irish Home Rule, having arrived at the same conclusion as Mazzini had reached much earlier: that no good ever ensued to rulers or ruled when one nation dominated another.

The Liberal party finally split over the Bill and Chamberlain resigned from the cabinet. In the end, when the Bill was read for

126

a second time in June, it was defeated by thirty votes—ninety Liberals, who now came to be known as Liberal-Unionists, having voted with the Tories. The Liberal government went to the country and were defeated in the ensuing General Election. The outcome of all this was that the Tories and so-called Liberal-Unionists (indistinguishable from the Tories) ruled Britain for twenty years, with the exception of a short-lived Liberal government under Gladstone's last premiership between 1892 and 1895.

The General Election campaign of 1885 was held during the last week of November and the beginning of December. Lloyd George's practice in public speaking during the preceding months had prepared him as a speaker for the Liberal party in this campaign. The real hero of the campaign in the eyes of Lloyd George and some of his fellow Radicals was Joseph Chamberlain and not Gladstone. This is evident from references to Chamberlain even before the campaign got fully under way:

1885
21 Oct. Meeting in Chwilog to pledge support to Gladstone and return of Liberal Government. Herber Evans there and delivered sweeping speech. His glowing reference to Chamberlain elicited 'Hurrahs'.

29 Oct. Llanaelhaiarn meeting. I got on very well. . . . Mr. Lumley [the Congregational Minister] praising my speech very much, *predicting I would make another Chamberlain.*

23 Nov. Port. meeting. I raised alternate roars of laughter and rounds of cheering. John Roberts in proposing a vote of thanks to the speakers singled me out as a future M.P. The audience cheered.

26 Nov. Further Tory victories—this is rather disheartening, I confess. It must be these Parnellites—humdrum Liberalism won't win elections. Llew Glas [a local grocer in Criccieth] warning me that they intended stoning J. Owen and myself on Saturday night.

Sat. 28 Nov. News of Gladstone's overwhelming victory last night. . . . Rowdy meeting at Criccieth. Meeting broke up. I was warned that rioters threatened to kill me.

Mon. 1 Dec. Some of our weak-kneed Liberal leaders decided not to hold meeting this evening. I was awfully annoyed at this—there were about 60 coming over from Porthmadog to assist in maintaining order.

4 Dec. Did some work in office but not much—Great Liberal victories in counties. Very glad of it. I am convinced that this is due to Chamberlain's speeches. Gladstone had no programme.

Just as Henry George's ideas on land ownership influenced Lloyd George's policy later as Chancellor of the Exchequer, so Joseph Chamberlain's speeches in 1885 made a profound impression on him. Several of the fiscal provisions in the Finance Act 1910 can be traced to some of Chamberlain's radical ideas. A good instance of Chamberlain's radicalism, which made such an appeal to Lloyd George and Liberals in Wales, is the following extract from a speech he delivered in London in 1885:

I want you not to accept as final, or as perfect, arrangements under which hundreds of thousands, nay millions, of your fellow countrymen are subject to untold misery with the evidence all round them of accumulated wealth and unbounded luxury. . . . I believe the great evil with which we have to deal is the excessive inequality in the distribution of riches.

Lloyd George did not 'bite' until 1909, but his bite can to some extent be connected with Joseph Chamberlain's bark a quarter of a century earlier.

By the end of 1885 the stage had been set for Lloyd George and several other ardent young Welshmen born in the second half of the nineteenth century to make their début on the political stage of Wales. The combined effect of the Reform and Redistribution Acts 1884–5 had enfranchised not only householders in rural areas but thousands of working-class voters, such as quarrymen in Gwynedd and miners in the South Wales valleys. Chamberlain had seen what Gladstone in his declining years had failed to realize—that the whole structure of political democracy in Britain had altered, and that in future any party or party leader would have to gain the support of these newly enfranchised voters in order to wield effective political power. Joseph Chamberlain was mainly responsible for drawing the attention of Welsh Radicals to this fundamental shift in the movement towards the creation of the modern state.

The effect of the electoral reform measures on Wales itself was dramatic and immediate as a result of the 1885 General Election: the Tories only retained four of the thirty-four Welsh seats, and only nine of these constituencies were now represented by members of the landed gentry. The new mood was reflected by the loss of prestige suffered by established Welsh Liberal leaders, such as Osborne Morgan, in the eyes of the younger generation of Liberals. After listening to Osborne Morgan speaking at Ffestiniog during the course of the election campaign, Lloyd George referred to his speech as: 'very superficial. No depth, no fervour'.

In early 1886, whilst uncertainty reigned in Westminster as to whether Salisbury's minority Tory government could remain in office, two apparently unconnected events occurred, both of which were to have an important bearing on Lloyd George's career. The first was the appointment by the Tory Lord Chancellor of a new County Court Judge, Judge Bishop, for the North Wales circuit. The significance of the new judge's appointment was the mutual antipathy between Lloyd George and Bishop, which became evident on Lloyd George's first appearances before him. Lloyd George's comments were:

The new Judge appears dreamy, slow & lacking in perspicacity. He does not have much affability in his address and I am apprehensive of him developing into a cantankerous old crony.

Port. County Court. Had a great number of cases there—Got on badly with Judge. I had some sharp tussles with him. . . . I told him that [this case] was very important for my clients who were poor, and that it was not a question of the length of the Affidavit but of doing justice between the parties. I also asked him not to form an opinion before he had heard both sides. I had two or three more sharp tussles with him in other cases. I cheeked him outright, and if he had in him a grain of dignity he would have resented it.

These appearances before Judge Bishop in 1886 were but preliminary skirmishes before battle was joined between them in earnest on the occasion of the Llanfrothen burial case in 1888. This case probably more than any other single occurrence made Lloyd George's name known throughout Wales as a champion of Welsh radicalism and nonconformity. At the end of January 1886, when the Tory government resigned, Lloyd George said he wished they had been defeated before Judge Bishop had been appointed. The irony of the appointment in reality was that the judge's strong prejudice against Lloyd George and most of what he said helped to sharpen Lloyd George's power of invective when he opposed the injustices meted out by the establishment.

The second significant event of this year was the meeting of the Irish Land League leader, Michael Davitt, at Blaenau Ffestiniog in February. Before this Lloyd George had spoken at an open Liberal Club meeting in Criccieth to an audience of about 150 in favour of forming a Land League in the area on the lines of the Irish Land League. The chairman remarked, 'Our friend Mr. George is pretty extreme as you know.' A few days after this meeting a Land League conference was convened and Lloyd George was appointed as one of the two Criccieth delegates. His supporter, Dr. Evans, was actively organizing a Land League

129

Association at Blaenau Ffestiniog and trying to get Lloyd George appointed chairman. A week earlier Lloyd George had met Bryn Roberts, who had just been elected to Parliament for the first time in the December 1885 election as Liberal member for one of the Caernarfonshire constituencies. He was lukewarm in his support for the Land League, and told Lloyd George that he did not believe the farmers would ever join such an extremist organization. Lloyd George replied that he believed the farmers would join if the Liberal leaders in North Wales took the movement in earnest.

When Lloyd George went to Michael Davitt's meeting at Blaenau Ffestiniog he met the man who, he once declared, was his 'most admired figure in real life'. Dr. Evans had invited him to speak at the meeting but he replied that he was unprepared and went to the meeting 'gnawing his fingers' that he had spent his time playing draughts at the Club instead of preparing a speech. The meeting that evening was chaired by the Reverend Michael Daniel Jones of Bala, who probably did more than any other Welsh leader of the last century to arouse amongst his fellow countrymen an awareness of their national identity. He inspired and took a leading part in organizing the movement which led to the founding of a Welsh colony in Patagonia in 1865. He despaired of any real progress being made towards the realization of his dream of an independent Welsh nation by the Welsh Liberal leaders of his own generation and had decided to put his faith in the rising generation of emerging political figures, such as T. E. Ellis and David Lloyd George. So at the opening of the Blaenau Ffestiniog meeting he announced that Lloyd George was to speak after Michael Davitt. The hall was packed; Lloyd George was astounded. He was in two minds whether he would speak or not. However, after listening to Michael Davitt, he retired to an ante-room and there 'amid the talk of some turbulent youth' he tried to prepare a speech.

As on many other occasions Lloyd George was inspired by his knowledge of the Bible to open his speech with a telling scriptural reference. He decided to couch his speech in the form of a vote of thanks to the *two Michaels*—Michael D. Jones, the chairman, and Michael Davitt, M.P., the guest speaker. He said that *one* Michael with his angels had thrown down that old serpent called Satan, but that night in Blaenau Ffestiniog they had *two* Michaels on their side. He declared, speaking throughout in Welsh, that there was no limit to what two Michaels would accomplish together on behalf of the underprivileged and downtrodden in their common struggle against the oppressor. This brought the house down.

After the meeting he went to Dr. Evans's house and had dinner with the two Michaels. Lloyd George recorded his impressions of the occasion:

Regarding Davitt, I am very favourably impressed by his presence. He appears to be very earnest and sincere—tho he spoke for about an hour he was listened to with unflagging interest. He highly complimented me—told me that I aroused by far the most enthusiasm—that it was quite evident I touched the heart of the audience. Although he could not understand me, he knew very well I was eloquent. . . . My speech gone like wild-fire through Ffestiniog—they're going to make me an M.P. Michael Jones for it. Long talk with him, Pan Jones and Mr. Davitt at the L. & N.W. Railway hotel—*scheming future of agitation—I feel I am in it now.*

The suggestion of getting him to stand as a Liberal candidate for Merioneth gained the support of the Ffestiniog quarrymen, but some of the leading ministers in the town and others raised doubts whether he had the means to stand for Parliament. Lloyd George commented: 'The election expenses are of course my great obstacle.' His further problem was that Members of Parliament in those days were not paid any salary, so he concluded that he should wait another five years 'before having a shot at Robertson', the sitting member.

After the resignation of Lord Salisbury's Tory administration, Gladstone once again became Prime Minister, and in April 1886 introduced a Bill for Irish Home Rule. The Liberal party was split over the issue. Parnell had alienated a great many of his English supporters by the vehemence with which he had attacked both Parliament and Englishmen in general.

Chamberlain's attitude was that he was prepared to support a much more limited form of Irish Home Rule than that proposed in Gladstone's Bill. He objected to granting full rights of taxation to Ireland and resisted the surrender by Britain of the right to appoint judges. When Gladstone refused to modify the Bill, Chamberlain resigned from the government. When the Bill was read for the second time in June 1886, it was defeated by 343 to 313, over 90 Liberals having voted with the Conservatives. The decisive factor which had led to the defeat of the Bill and the resignation of Gladstone's administration, following the defeat, had been Joseph Chamberlain's opposition and resignation from the cabinet.

The leaders of Welsh Liberalism during the months preceding and after the fall of Gladstone's administration remained loyal to him. After his success at Blaenau Ffestiniog Lloyd George had been invited to join them when they met for private discussions and such a meeting took place in Bangor during the Easter week-end. The Liberal leaders believed that Chamberlain had been moved by entirely selfish aims in the matter. Lloyd George said that he did not agree with them, and found himself to be a minority of one in sticking up for Chamberlain. He recorded that Chamberlain's speeches in Parliament on the Irish Home Rule Bill was 'a thorough masterpiece—very convincing and clear'. However, when addressing a public meeting in Merioneth on the Home Rule issue a few days later, he was rather dismayed to discover that the 'thoroughly Chamberlainian resolution' he had drawn up was received without acclamation, when put by him to the meeting. He addressed several meetings in Merioneth during the period of the run-up to the July 1886 General Election. Several delegates to the meetings held in Dolgellau and Bala to select a Liberal candidate wanted him to stand, but he stated emphatically that he 'would not in any way go against Ellis' chances'. He was then pressed to allow his name to go forward if T. E. Ellis could not raise the necessary funds. Lloyd George said:

Foolishly promised to do so. When alone and calculating the possible consequences and ways & means I regretted my temerity, but have found way of getting the cash as I think—by getting friends to guarantee fund in Bank—but I would not be in nearly as good a position as regards pecuniary—oratorical or intellectual capacity to go to Parliament now as in say 5 years hence. Now I would put myself in endless pecuniary difficulties—an object of contempt in a House of snobs. Besides I am not yet as thoroughly established in judgment as I ought to be.

T. E. Ellis's financial problem was solved, and Lloyd George withdrew his name, with the result that Ellis was adopted and subsequently fought and won the election as the Liberal member for his native county of Merioneth. He gained a majority of 1,267 votes over his Conservative opponent John Vaughan. In his letter thanking the electors of Merioneth for returning him to Parliament he said that Wales, like Ireland, would face many enemies in the new Parliament. Unlike most of his fellow Liberal candidates he had openly supported Home Rule for Wales, and in effect identified the two countries as having one common crusade in which they should join forces against an alien government in London. Gladstonian Liberals did well in Wales in the 1886 General Election, but they were badly defeated in England, and in the new House there were only 191 Gladstonian Liberals and 81 Irish Nationalists against 316 Conservatives and 78 Liberal-Unionists under Chamberlain's leadership. As the election results came in Lloyd

George's faith in Chamberlain appeared to be as strong as ever, and he would have liked to have seen him 'hold the balance between the parties'. In supporting Chamberlain Lloyd George was taking an independent line amongst his fellow Liberals and was also out of step in his uncle's eyes. Before the election Richard Lloyd wrote in his diary: '*April 14, 1886:* What a pity Chamberlain is astray.' When the Irish Home Rule Bill came up for its second reading, Richard Lloyd attributed to Chamberlain the responsibility for splitting the Liberal party. He added: 'G.P.W. [one of Lloyd George's staunchest early supporters in Criccieth] told me this morning that D.Ll.G must be careful or he would be accused of being against the Party.'

Going by Lloyd George's openly expressed views before and during the 1886 election, had he been selected as the Liberal candidate for Merioneth and won, he would, it appears, have been sitting with the Liberal-Unionists under Joseph Chamberlain. The reason for this is not far to seek: he regarded Chamberlain as the out-and-out Radical whose attacks on the aristocracy had won his youthful heart. Chamberlain was a Unitarian, like James Martineau, his father's Liverpool friend, and was more concerned with improving the material conditions of life of the newly enfranchised voters than in spending all his energies in trying to solve the almost insoluble political situation in Ireland. T. E. Ellis was more orthodox in reflecting the views of his party than Lloyd George. But, though he had apparently experienced difficulty in raising funds to contest the election, he had never been a poor man. His father was a tenant-farmer of sufficient substance to send his son for four years to the University of Wales College at Aberystwyth, and thereafter to Oxford. Lloyd George, on the other hand, had experienced what poverty meant to a family—the phantoms of illness and shortage of ready cash had far too frequently haunted the Llanystumdwy and Criccieth homes. It was this experience which in later years gave such a keen edge to his assaults upon the citadels of established and inherited wealth and the power that went with such wealth. Chamberlain lost his radical fervour within a few years of becoming a Liberal-Unionist, and his bark in the cause of the under-privileged never developed into a bite. Nevertheless Lloyd George's determination from an early age to make drastic social reform his first priority had been greatly strengthened and inspired by the Chamberlain of 1885 and 1886 though his disenchantment with Chamberlain was complete before he entered Parliament in 1890.

T. E. Ellis and Lloyd George were to dominate the Welsh political scene between 1890 and Ellis's untimely death in 1899.

In 1886 with his election to Parliament Ellis became the fore-runner, and as the excitement of the election subsided Lloyd George probably realized he had been in too much of a hurry in allowing his name to be considered as a candidate. Richard Lloyd told him that it was essential that he should get his solicitor's business firmly established as a solid foundation for any further advancement and his good friend Dr. Evans told him not to be in too much of a hurry and that 'his turn would surely come'. With his political interest now thoroughly aroused he was during most of 1885 and 1886 straining hard to slip the leash which held him to the legal practice in Porthmadog and Criccieth. In his heart of hearts he did not believe that the law and politics went well to-gether. When I was a law student in 1933 and staying with him at Churt I remember asking him his views on the relationship be-tween the law as a profession and politics. He replied that the law tended to inhibit the politician from ever developing into a states-man and reaching the heights. I asked him to explain, and he then instanced men like F. E. Smith (Lord Birkenhead), Lord Reading and John Simon, all of them men of the most brilliant intellect and persuasive speakers, but none of them memorable as statesmen. 'The truth is', he said, 'that a lawyer is taught from the beginning to speak on behalf of someone else—a solicitor is bound by his instructions and a barrister by his brief. To succeed as a politician you must say what you yourself think.' He added that he had observed that John Simon, in particular, when speaking in the House of Commons always gave the impression that he held a brief in his hands, and that one was never quite sure what the man himself really thought.

The law is certainly a demanding and possessive profession, and Lloyd George's apparent determination that its demands on him should be as light as possible arose from an early intuition of the threat a legal career could be to his political advancement. He feared that if he carried on unassisted he would be overwhelmed by the responsibility of his profession. In February 1886, he entered in his diary:

Pressing William to join me. Have more points of law to decide in a week than Breese, Jones & Casson have in a year.

His brother was then in the fourth year of his articles with Breese, Jones & Casson, and due to sit his final and honours examinations in April 1887. I shudder to think what the effect on my father's prospects would have been if he had succumbed to this pressure in 1886, and found himself, before having had the oppor-tunity to qualify as a solicitor, to all intents and purposes working as a full-time executive in his brother's expanding legal practice. He was already working in double harness and assisting his brother out of office hours. My father told me that it was largely due to Randall Casson's refusal to release him that he was enabled to complete his legal studies, making full use of the complete set of law reports and legal textbooks at the office of Breese, Jones & Casson. He made good use of the opportunity for study afforded by this office and his principal and in April 1887 passed his final examination and was placed fourth in the first class in the honours examination—a brilliant achievement.

Lloyd George kept up the pressure in his anxiety to get William to join him—during William's last year of articles, if possible, but failing that, as soon as he had qualified. According to his diary this is how William himself viewed the situation in February 1886:

If D. were to co-operate with me and continue on his own for 12 months, I should then be pretty safe of a good place, I believe; but I almost think he cannot. To-night he was full of the money which he could make if he attended properly to the businesses he had received this year. I retired after 12, having entered up David's cash-book, and had a chat about different matters with him. He had 14 letters to go out to-day.

With William remaining at Breese, Jones & Casson's office, Lloyd George enrolled the assistance of his uncle Lloyd to help out with the clerical work. At the age of fifty, with some reluctance, Richard Lloyd agreed to familiarize himself with the technical terms of the solicitor's language. This is how Lloyd George described one of his uncle's earliest efforts as a process-server:

Sending uncle to Bala to serve writ. He was most unwilling to go,— in fact, almost crying over it. I pitied him sorely while laughing at his anguish—he came home by 4 train having accomplished his task triumphantly. He appears highly elated at his success, especially when William & I join to praise his ingenuity and tact. Poor fellow—he is oversensitive and retirement has conduced to this condition. This is the way to cure him. His success on this occasion will embolden him.

This initial success did in fact embolden Richard Lloyd at the outset of his appointment as solicitor's clerk, and he remained a faithful servant of the firm for many years. On the front page of his diary for 1887 Richard Lloyd wrote:

Diary for Office Purposes
Gweithio yng ngoleuni y dyfodol pell.
(Working in the light of the distant future.)

135

I don't heed but as little as possible present popularity, which only lasts two years or so, but I write with an eye on 1951. (Macaulay in a letter to H. Rogers: 1851.)

This revealing entry shows that Richard Lloyd knew perfectly well what he was about in recording the calls and messages at the Criccieth office, and seeing that they received the professional attention of one or other of the two brothers.

The problem of running his legal practice on a shoe-string was not the only problem to occupy Lloyd George's mind during 1886–7. He had been endowed with an abundance of virility, and since his teens he had been sought after by the girls as an extremely vivacious and attractive companion. His affair with Liza Jones, the singer, was the first one in which his feelings had been deeply engaged. Even after it had come to an end, and he had burnt her letters to him, their inevitable occasional encounters continued to trouble him. Like him she was a Baptist, and her voice was outstanding during the hymn-singing in the Sunday services.

1884

18 June I wish to God she would keep away altogether. I might feel it keenly, perhaps, for a while, but I'd sooner get over it by not seeing her at all than by being compelled, as I am now, to see her and *hear her voice* twice a week.

In a later diary entry he took comfort in the fact that had he married her, 'it would cost between £200 & £300 to train in the Royal Academy of Music'.

It is not likely that I shall be in a position to do this for her for many a year yet, and certainly not without the knowledge of my uncle to whom I am attached beyond anyone I have yet met.

Lloyd George had first met Margaret Owen of Mynydd Ednyfed, Criccieth in June 1884 and had commented in his diary then, 'Maggie Owen . . . there—she is a sensible girl without fuss or affectation about her', but there is no reference to a further meeting until May 1885, when under the auspices of the Criccieth Debating Society a 'grand soirée' was held:

A really 1st class affair—the victualling part as excellent as the entertainment—playing forfeits and the like games until 11.30. About 30 present. Took Maggie Owen home a short way—her mother waiting for her in some house. Had my new suit.

This reference to Maggie's mother intervening to cut short his walk home with her was more significant than he realized at the time. Margaret Owen was the only child of Richard and Mary Owen and Mynydd Ednyfed was a farm in a superb position on the crest of the hill to the north of Criccieth. Richard Owen was regarded in the farming community as a man of sound judgement, and his services were frequently called upon as a valuer. There is no higher compliment to a farmer than the trust which is placed in him by a colleague to value his stock when he takes up—or surrenders—possession of his farm. Richard Owen was also a prosperous farmer in his own right, and he had sent Margaret to be educated at Dr. Williams's school for girls at Dolgellau. The main object of this school in those days was to train the girls to be genteel young ladies, and the open use of the Welsh language was frowned upon. Eluned Morgan, the Welsh South American writer, was a pupil at Dr. Williams's school at about the same time and years later, in 1909, visited Margaret in London when she was the wife of the Chancellor of the Exchequer. In a letter to William George she said, 'The afternoon I spent with Mrs. Lloyd George has been an uplifting experience for me. I have seen how a character bred amongst the mountains has been able to remain undefiled by the world, although in the midst of chaotic conditions.' This is a revealing comment on Margaret Owen's essential character—she was a quietly self-assured and dignified personality, with a strong sense of humour, but she was devoid of worldly ambition and accordingly unable to share instinctively in her future husband's dream of getting on in the world and carving out for himself an outstanding political career. She was not prepared to allow her sense of propriety or her priorities to be upset by even so strong a personality as David Lloyd George.

Margaret's father, Richard Owen, was a deacon in the Calvinistic Methodist church which met at Capel Mawr, and Margaret had been brought up to take her full part in the life of the chapel. She remained a faithful member of the Calvinistic Methodist connexion throughout her life, and it is no wonder that amongst those who wanted to marry her was the Reverend John Owen, M.A., the Minister of Capel Mawr, and subsequently of Capel Seion, Criccieth. When a split occurred in the Capel Mawr membership John Owen and some of the senior deacons, including Richard Owen, were given permission by the central denominational committee to build a second chapel in Criccieth. The strength of sectarian feeling in Wales at that period can be inferred from the fact that a split could occur in a chapel where all the members were of the same denomination. Between different denominations the rivalry was often acute, and on a marriage taking place between members of two different denominations problems would arise such as whether

137

the wife should change her denomination so that husband and wife could worship together and bring up their family in the same church. Members of the numerically small denominations, such as the Baptists, believed that both in business and public life they suffered from a degree of discrimination against them, and there were often sound grounds for their belief. When Lloyd George set out to court Margaret Owen, as a member of the Baptist chapel in Criccieth, he was under a distinct handicap.

During the summer of 1885 Margaret Owen and Lloyd George met on two or three occasions quite casually. For instance both were members of a day excursion party to Ynys Enlli (Bardsey Island):

13 July Fine. At 9 with steamer Snowdon for a trip to Bardsey— about 16 altogether going from Criccieth. It was a picnic party organised by some one from Portmadoc. I with Miss Owen, Mynydd Edynfed, mostly. M.E.G. (my sister) with us—Enjoyed myself immensely.

At the end of 1885 Lloyd George cut out and inserted in his diary the following from a newspaper's advertisement column:

Matrimony. A lady aged 21, medium height, fair, blue eyes, golden hair, considered very prepossessing and of a very affectionate nature with private income of £800 p.a., would like to hear from a nice gentleman, wanting a loving wife. Address: Miss Tempsford, c/o Editor, 40 Lamb's Conduit, London, W.C.

History does not relate whether or not he cut this out with a view to responding to this alluring invitation, but early in 1886 he decided that he would court Margaret Owen in earnest.

1886
7 Jan. Very glad I waylaid Maggie Owen; induced her to abstain from going to the Seiat [evening service] by showing her by my erratic watch that she was too late, then for a stroll with her up Lôn Fêl [Lovers' Lane].

4 Feb. At 6 p.m. met Maggie Owen by appointment on the Marine Parade. With her until 7. I am getting to be very fond of the girl. There is a combination of good nature, humour and affection about her.

7 Feb. After dinner with W.G. [William George] along Abereistedd and thence to chapel. Mentioned my predicament with regard to love affairs. He does not disapprove.

9 Feb. At 5.45 attended Burial Board meeting, thence to an ap-
138

pointed rendezvous by 6.30 at Bryn Hir gate to meet Maggie Owen; took her home by round-about way, enjoyed the stroll immensely and made another appointment. It looks as if I were rapidly placing myself in an irretrievable position. Doesn't matter. I don't see that any harm will ensue. Left her at 7.45.

15 Feb. (After concert) I then waylaid Maggie Owen to take her home. Never felt more acutely than to-night that I am really in deep love with girl. Felt sorry to have to leave her. I have I know gradually got to like her more and more. There's another thing I have observed in connection with this, that my intercourse with L. rather tended to demoralize my taste; my fresh acquaintance has an entirely different influence. She firmly checks all ribaldry or tendency thereto on my part.

16 Feb. Met Maggie Owen—with her till 8. She will not stay any longer.

4 March Went up to meet M. Whilst talking to her, she had to leave to go to Seiat.

9 March Up to meet M. Walked in public with her without a blush. . . . *Think I have at last made a prudent choice.*

11 June Met M. First time I ever used an expression of endearment towards her. Feel I am becoming very fond of her.

26 June Mynydd Ednyfed servant girl came here to tell me that M. ill in bed. Determined to go up to-morrow evening. Told servant so.

27 June After making a feint of running for train, envelope in hand, started via sea-wall and Turnpike, Criccieth, for the hills. M. expecting me. M. asked me what I would tell them at home if they wanted to know where I'd been. I replied: 'I'd say I'd been to see my sweet-heart.' This is the second time I've called her so. She likes it. I am now quite committed.

18 July Sunday. After evening service happened to see Maggie, followed her up to Mynydd Ednyfed, with her then down to road by Turnpike—who should I meet coming down there but J.R., Uncle and Wm. Williams—jumped over wall and hid behind Turnpike cottage.

22 July Told my sister M.E.G. to-night about M. She is well-pleased and thinks a lot of her, says I may mention the matter (of proposing) to M. shortly but that it would not do to marry for about five years at least.

Over the August Bank Holiday week-end that year Lloyd George went to London with the Garn schoolmaster, Lloyd Williams, who was later to marry Liza Jones, the singer. He went to the Lyceum on the Saturday evening to hear Irving acting Mephistopheles in *Faust*. On the Monday they went to the Colonial Exhibition, but he said there were too many good things to be able to enjoy any, and in the evening they went to see *The Mikado*. Shortly after returning from London, Lloyd George was told by a mutual acquaintance that Margaret Owen feared very much that he was a flirt, and that after winning her affection she would be let down by him. This friend then added that Margaret was already very fond of him. Lloyd George commented: 'This remark gave me deep joy.'

Towards the end of August Margaret went to stay with relatives of hers at Llanwnda, near Caernarfon. Lloyd George records in detail the circumstances in which he proposed to her, and how she responded.

1886

25 Aug. Left Caernarfon per 4.40 train—dropped down at Llanwnda. Wrote at the Inn at Llanwnda a note for her . . . marched right up to the door (where she was staying), asked if Miss Owen was in, told the girl at the door that I was desired by her father Richard Owen to give her a note in passing! Eventually I saw her. It appears Miss Jones had read the note, M, being too excited to open it. She had to go to a party that evening, but promised to try and return by 8, and to meet me by the gate; I gave her a bouquet I had brought with me. . . . I returned at 8 to Bodfan—but had to wait until 9.45 until the girls returned. M came with me for a long drive in carriage (I had brought from Llanwnda). Here I proposed to her. She wanted time to consider, but admitted her regard for me. Although, when I write this, I have not been formally accepted, I am positive that everything is all right so far as the girl is concerned. I left her about mid-night. M. has some of the 'coquette' about her—she did not like to appear to jump at my offer.

Margaret Owen did not give her reply for some time to Lloyd George, and this delay in obtaining an affirmative response from her made him into a more ardent suitor than ever. He would be out late at night and Richard Lloyd worried as to the whereabouts of his favourite nephew. He even took to walking around Criccieth to look for Lloyd George, and to asking passers-by whether they had seen him anywhere. Lloyd George was naturally extremely annoyed at this avuncular intrusion into his private affairs, and to put an end to his uncle's late-night walks, he hid his boots! Lloyd George was very much in love with Margaret by this time, and quite determined to win her, having thrown to the wind his sister's advice that he should wait another five years at least. Richard Owen and his wife would not allow Margaret to bring him to Mynydd Ednyfed, and accordingly he was only able to meet her there when, on rare occasions, both her parents happened to be away. Such an occasion occurred on 1 October 1886, and Lloyd George recorded in his diary:

To Mynydd Ednyfed & Mr and Mrs Owen having gone to Ty Mawr. I remained until 1 a.m. I pressed M. to come to a point as to what I had been speaking to her about (proposal of marriage). She at last admitted that her hesitation was entirely due to her not being able implicitly to trust me. She then asked me solemnly whether I was really in earnest. I assured her with equal solemnity that I was as there is a God in Heaven. 'Well then,' she said, 'if you will be as true and faithful to me as I am to you, it will be all right.'

At the end of October Margaret was off to London for a holiday. Lloyd George wrote to her, and told her to go to the Lyceum to see *Faust*, and 'if you want an exquisitely funny comedy go to the Savoy to see *The Mikado*'. Unfortunately, after her return to Criccieth from London the path of true love was still not running smoothly, and Margaret apparently still wanted the affair to be kept as clandestine as possible:

13 Nov. After dinner went over to meet M. by appointed trysting place. William Roberts, Penystumllyn, taking her home from Penystumllyn. I stuck to my post until he came up. Maggie rather angry I did not hide myself—but I stood to my dignity. Rather strong rebuke from M. for having condescended to gabble at all with Plas Wilbraham girls. I foolishly let out somehow that I had done so—she let me off—dismissed me—in disgrace.

This reprimand by Margaret followed close on the heels of a meeting they had had two days earlier, when they had met by Parciau gate in Criccieth, and Lloyd George recorded in his diary:

Never on better terms. *First time she ever gave me a kiss.* She gave it in exchange for a story I promised to tell her.

We do not know what the story was that prompted the bestowal of this kiss, but it seems that Lloyd George's proposal of marriage to Margaret preceded their first kiss by several weeks! At the beginning of November 1886 Lloyd George, in his letters to Margaret, addressed her as 'My dear Miss Owen'. In the first letter he wrote after she had kissed him for the first time he addressed her as 'My dearest Miss Owen'. He did not address her by her Christian name until February 1887.

He became concerned that Margaret's relatives and her mother were influencing her to keep away from him, presumably in the hope that he would lose interest in such a slowly developing love affair. In his letters he pressed her to turn up at their appointed trysting place, and 'not to be led away by any cousins, aunts, uncles or other next-of-kin'. At about this time a breach of promise of marriage claim was brought by Miss Annie Jones, a sister of Liza Jones the singer, against Lloyd George's cousin, John Jones of Caerdyni. Lloyd George accepted instructions from Annie Jones. On any view it was surprising that he should have accepted instructions against his own cousin and one who had helped the family during the lean years, but he may have thought that by doing so he could negotiate a softer settlement than would be the case if another solicitor were to act on behalf of Miss Jones, though he would then hardly be doing his duty to the claimant. Criccieth is a small town, and it was of course well known that Lloyd George had had an affair with Liza Jones. Moreover these were clearly no ordinary instructions, as they involved visits to the home of his former girl-friend. Margaret Owen was naturally put out by his determination to carry on with the case, and it was not surprising that his action in sending her Anne Jones's letter to read, in an attempt to reassure her that his only interest in the matter was professional, failed in its object. Margaret Owen's reply shows, reading between the lines, how deeply she was in love with him by this time in spite of the formal way she couched the beginning and end of her letter. It is one of the few letters she wrote him which have survived and serves to throw fresh light on their relationship at this crisis point in their courtship.

My dear Mr George,

I have begged of them to let me come to Portmadoc this evening, but father has utterly refused to let me go. I am sure I don't know why, therefore I must submit to his will and stay at home. I trust you will get this note in time. I am returning you the girl's letter. After reflecting upon what you told me yesterday I must tell you that I should much prefer your leaving it to some one else to take up; not because of your relationship to the man nor to let him go unpunished by any means for he really deserves it, but for your own sake. All the old stories will be renewed again. I know there are relatives of mine at Criccieth, and other people as well, who will be glad to have anything more to say to my people about you, to set them against you and that will put me in an awkward position. I know this much, I shall not be at my ease while the thing is on, if you will be taking it up. If she were a stranger to you, and you took her case, people would wonder why on earth you took it against your cousin, knowing that your relations were against your doing so; but now they will draw different conclusions—that you are on friendly terms with these people. . . .

Let some one else do it. You can get plenty of excuses; *one* that your people are against you doing it and recommend some other lawyer. Should your reputation depend upon it, as you said, that would only be from a professional point of view, not from any other point of view, I can assure you. . . . Yours faithfully,

M. OWEN

Looking back over the shoulder of the years it seems almost incredible that Lloyd George really believed that his professional reputation depended on him clinging on to these instructions, which, as Margaret rightly pointed out to him, should have been passed to some one else. I believe that his reluctance to do so sprang from his determination to have his own way. He generally got his own way at home, and anyone who had the effrontery to thwart him in his chosen line of action tended to come in for a drubbing.

Breach of promise actions were not at all uncommon in those days, and the possibility, remote as it was, that he might become involved in a claim by Margaret may have crossed his mind, because in November 1886 he started keeping in a notebook a carbon copy of each of the letters he wrote her. In some of these letters he adopted a scolding and sometimes openly aggressive tone, singling out Mrs. Owen in particular for criticism and blaming her for showing narrow sectarianism in her attitude towards him. By writing in this way he knew that Margaret would have to be in love with him if she decided to continue to meet him. On 19 January 1887 he sent her two letters he had just received from T. E. Ellis, whom the Owens respected highly. He wrote:

When may I see you? Write to let me know. I enclose the two last letters I received from T. Ellis. It would do your mother good to read these letters as it will bring home to her mind that it is not perhaps essential to even good Methodism that you should taboo other sectarians. *Darllenwch nhw i'ch mam bendith tad i chi.* [Read them to your mother for goodness sake.] She'll pull as wry a face as if she were drinking a gallon of assafatida.* Did you tell her what a scandal she has created about us throughout Lleyn?

Sincerest love from Your ever
D. Lloyd George.

* Asafoetida was a herb-drink with a rather horrible smell, much used to cure various stomach ailments in those days.

143

On 26 January he wrote to a Porthmadog jeweller enclosing a finger card, and stating that the size of the rings he required to see was No. 7. He added: 'Send off for a few *to-day* without fail—I want them by Friday.' But Margaret Owen was in no mood then to become formally engaged and she wrote Lloyd George a letter, which he termed an 'ultimatum', apparently upbraiding him for making his breach of promise case a pretext to visit Liza Jones at her home. Lloyd George replied indignantly, obviously believing that Margaret was paying too much heed to the gossip of busybodies. 'There is nothing wrong', he said, 'in being entertained with a little harmless music by a couple of girls, whom a bevy of dried-up, desiccated and blighted old maids object to.' They were clients and members of the same chapel as him. 'One of the few religious dogmas of our creed I believe in is—fraternity, with which you may couple Equality. My God never decreed that farmers and their race should be esteemed beyond the progeny of a fishmonger; strange to say, Christ—the founder of our creed— selected the missionaries of his noble teaching from among fishmongers. Do you really think that the Christ who honoured and made friendship with Zebedeus the fishmonger's son would disdain the acquaintance of a poor toiling fishwoman's daughter?' (The mother of Anne and Liza Jones ran a fishmonger's business in Criccieth.) At the close of his letter, with characteristic defiance, he took up the gauntlet which Margaret had cast before him: 'You ask me to choose—I have made my choice deliberately & solemnly —I must now ask you to make your choice. I know my slanderers— those whom you allow to poison your mind against me. Choose between them and me—there can be no other alternative. May I see you at 7 to-morrow?'

He described the note he received in reply as 'rather disappointing', but in it she suggested a further meeting. Lloyd George somewhat curtly replied, agreeing to a further meeting and adding: 'It is time you should cast off your swaddling clothes.'

Under these epistolary onslaughts she remained dignified and unruffled outwardly—an abiding characteristic of hers fortunately for Lloyd George; the more militant he became, the cooler her response!

His next letter to her was written in the early hours of a Sunday morning towards the end of January 1887. It was a frank and uninhibited letter, abrasive in tone occasionally, complaining of broken appointments (three in one week), and pointing out that he was 'quite entangled and confounded with office arrears'. He appealed to her for a little sympathy in his struggle to get on and then declared,

144

It comes to this, my supreme idea is to get on. To this idea I shall sacrifice everything—except I trust honesty. I am prepared to thrust even love itself under the wheels of my Juggernaut if it obstructs the way. . . . Do you not really desire my success? Recollect my success probably means yours. . . .

After that warning to Margaret Owen of what marriage to him would entail, he declared: 'My love to you is sincere and strong. In this I never waver, but I must not forget that I have a purpose in life, and however painful the sacrifice I have to make to attain this ambition I must not flinch.' At the foot of the letter he signed, 'From your sweetheart D.Ll.G.' He made it clear to her in another letter of this period:

I disdain the idea of lurking like a burglar about premises when I merely seek to obtain an honest interview with my sweetheart, and I have the same contempt for myself when I have been kicking my heels on the highway and lying in ambuscade like a footpad for half an hour, more or less, vainly expecting the performance of a definite promise of a stroll with my girl.

Lloyd George then received the following note from his sweetheart:

Mynydd Ednyfed,
Criccieth.

Dearest David,
I will be by the cemetery [on the road from Criccieth to Mynydd Ednyfed] this evening at 7 p.m. without fail.

Yours with love,
Maggie.

Lloyd George kept this note in his notebook with the copy letters. The 'Dearest David' and 'Yours with love Maggie' spoke for themselves, after the 'Mr. George' and 'Yours faithfully M. Owen' of the earlier note. The notes, incidentally, were almost invariably delivered by the Mynydd Ednyfed servant-girl. The path of true love was running smoothly at last, and Lloyd George knew now that her answer to his proposal of marriage would be favourable. The placing of the engagement ring on her finger would be a formality. Once he was engaged he came to the conclusion that the sooner he could get married the better. According to the entries in his 1887 diary* Mrs. Owens's relatives had still

---

* Deposited at the National Library of Wales: the Carey-Evans collection of the Lloyd George papers.

not abandoned their attempt to get at Margaret through her mother and influence her to give him up:

1887

22 March It occurs that the Misses Roberts of Bronygadair and Ystumllyn have been reviling me to Mrs. Owen—told her that they are surprised how I could stand in my shoes when I had been courting *'merch Nansi penwaig'* [Nansi the herring's daughter]. . . . Told M. that if her parents contrived to get at her in that style that the only way to put an end to it was to get married.

In his understandable desire to get married and put an end to their secretive meetings, he tended to underestimate the financial and other problems which would inevitably arise if he were to marry before he had established himself. His sister had some months previously advised him that he should wait for about five years, but in April he had another talk with her:

Walk with M.E.G. past Ynysgain farm—Told her my ideas as to getting married, that I wanted to pay Uncle his £200 first and then directly I am remunerated another £300—told her that if I were to complete matters in hand, I should probably get about £500 for them, and that W.G. could collect them in about 6 months. . . . She didn't in any way dissuade me.

William George was sitting his final examination that April, and Lloyd George thought his sister might have disapproved his plans for an early marriage inasmuch as his ability to marry so soon depended on their younger brother joining him and accepting financial responsibility in running the business. Lloyd George was the favoured child of the family and everyone took it for granted that William's lot in life was to be literally his brother's keeper. If Uncle Lloyd thought that William was not being as helpful to David as he should have been in his opinion, he lost no time in telling him so. Apparently it did not occur to Mary Ellen, the oldest of the three children, to ask David Lloyd, as he was called by his contemporaries, whether it was in William's interest that he should be drawn into his elder brother's newly established and struggling business immediately after he had passed his final examination, and before he had time to breathe. On Friday, 6 May 1887, a telegram arrived announcing that William George had passed his final examination, and on Tuesday, 10 May Lloyd George recorded in his diary that: 'W.G. went over to Breese, Jones & Casson to bid farewell. With me in afternoon, helping in office.' A few days later a telegram arrived to announce that 'W.G. had won first-class honours. Bravo Will—he thoroughly deserves

146

it.' If it was not fully apparent then, it was soon to become apparent what 'helping in the office' entailed for William. It was not a case of a younger brother joining his older brother to run a solicitors' practice to which they would both be dedicating the major portion of their time and energy, as is customary between business partners. To Lloyd George the practice was from the start an economic base for advancing his career, and he wished to be released as far as possible and as soon as possible from the day-to-day responsibility of running that practice.

The summer of 1887 progressed and William became more and more responsible for the work of the brothers' firm. Meanwhile Lloyd George's relationship with his daughter was not the only problem to trouble Richard Owen. He was one of the senior deacons at Capel Mawr, Criccieth—a large chapel, as its name implies and considered large enough to provide a meeting-place for the Methodists of Criccieth for the foreseeable future. According to contemporary records there had been rumblings of discontent amongst the Criccieth Methodists for some years, arising mainly from a difference of opinion as to the provision to be made for the English-speaking nonconformists who came to settle in Criccieth in increasing numbers after the railway had been extended to the town in about 1867. During the summer months in particular, visitors from England came to stay in the town, and a second Methodist chapel to provide a meeting place for the English-speaking Methodists and nonconformists was built some time before 1887. There had been a difference of opinion as to whether an 'English Chapel' (Capel Seisnig), should be built in Criccieth to provide for the newcomers to the district, and this difference of opinion reflected a general disagreement amongst Welsh non-conformists of the period, especially in South Wales, as to whether or not it was their duty to Christianize the English-speaking immigrants who were pouring into Wales at that time. Welsh nonconformity was and still is to some extent the principal protector of the Welsh language. The argument against building chapels to house the 'English cause' can be summed up by the following paragraph in the *Cardiff Times* of 30 November 1860, reporting an address on the subject by the prominent Welsh Liberal M.P., Henry Richard:

By the building of chapels, and the transferring of Welshmen to the assistance of those chapels, they were obliged to do something which tended to . . . destroy the Welsh language.

Like many of the leaders of Welsh thought at that time he believed that this was a necessary sacrifice on the part of Welsh nonconformity in order to save the souls of their English-speaking brethren in the faith, and Criccieth was among the seaside resorts which built a subsidiary chapel to the main one. After the English cause had been established Capel Mawr remained outwardly a united church under the ministry of the Reverend John Owen, but during the spring and summer of 1887 acute differences, the exact cause of which cannot now be discovered, but which were more or less of a personal nature, arose amongst the members, and these came to a head in August 1887. The governing body of the Calvinistic Methodist Church in North Wales then appointed a special committee to 'give the closest attention to the cause of the disagreements and quarrels which exist and have existed in the Criccieth church, with a view to restoring peace to this church'. In spite of the pleas made by the governing body's representatives harmony was not restored, and the outcome was that the church membership split down the middle, with the Reverend John Owen, Mr. and Mrs. Richard Owen and approximately half the members seceding from Capel Mawr. They decided to build a second Methodist chapel in Criccieth, and in the meantime were granted permission to hold their services at the English chapel, which had already been built. In fact, the seceding members assumed full responsibility for the English chapel, and it remained under the wing of Seion chapel which was then built. The partition of the membership of Capel Mawr in 1887-8 brought peace and harmony to the Methodists in Criccieth, a fact noted with satisfaction by the governing body at its meeting in Machynlleth in April 1888. It was Lloyd George's first lesson in partition, and how it can as a last resort bring a measure of harmony to a community no longer able to live in peace together. His sympathy at the time was wholly with the Reverend John Owen and his senior deacon, Richard Owen; he lost no time in making his views known to Margaret, and through her to Mr. and Mrs. Owen, and I have no doubt that his attitude on this burning issue of the day in Criccieth was welcomed by Mr. and Mrs. Owen, helping him substantially to gain approved entrance to Margaret's home for the first time.

1887

7 Sept. Up to Mynydd Ednyfed at 8. The old chap was out. I went in through front-door to drawing-room. Mrs. Owen told Maggie that I must not come more than 3 times a week. When Maggie replied that she would see me out the other nights, Mrs. Owen said: 'Na, rhaid i ti roi dy reswm ar waith.' [No, you must use your common sense.]

Margaret also told him that summer that she had received three proposals of marriage, including one from the Reverend John

148

Owen. On her showing him the letters Lloyd George commented: 'Cannot help admiring the honour and lack of brag which caused the girl not to show these letters to me ere this.' One of the other suitors was a deacon in the opposite camp. He was John Thomas Jones, a local landowner. He remained a bachelor, but John Owen, who was sixteen years older than Margaret, married a girl from the Vale of Clwyd in 1896. At the end of September it was agreed that David and Margaret should marry the following year—not later than the spring. This was after she had written him to say she had 'a scolding for staying up late last night'. She added:

My parents are angry with me one day and you another. I am on bad terms with one or the other continually. . . . Well I am very miserable, that is all I have to say, dearest Dei, and I hope things won't be long as they are now. Yours, MAG.

Lloyd George also decided in the autumn of 1887 that he would join the Independents' denomination and go to live at Porthmadog. Margaret Owen approved of his plan, 'the Capel Mawr verdict having disgusted her with Methodism'. He also told his brother who said he did not blame him if his 'views were so'. If Capel Mawr were still an acceptable venue for the marriage no problem would have arisen over the choice of a chapel for the wedding. But nothing came of the idea of joining the Congregationalists or Independents, and Lloyd George was in no position to set up a home for himself at Porthmadog or anywhere else in 1888. Eventually it was settled that the marriage should take place on 24 January 1888 in a small country chapel a few miles from Criccieth. This was a compromise, Richard Owen having said that he was too much of a Methodist to agree to a marriage at any chapel other than a Methodist chapel. Richard Lloyd was not told of the plan until a fortnight before the ceremony. He was faced with a *fait accompli*, but as it was David's doing he accepted the inevitable with good grace, and agreed to officiate at the wedding, provided it was conducted with the minimum of fuss and as privately as possible. He himself had not then met Margaret, but he recorded in his diary: *Mae pawb yn dweud ei bod yn eneth fwyn, synhwyrol ac yn eneth ddefnyddiol.* [Everyone says she is a pleasant, sensible girl and a practical girl.] To underline what a private affair the marriage was I need only add that on the bridegroom's side only Lloyd George and Uncle Lloyd went to the ceremony. The Reverend John Owen read a chapter, and Richard Lloyd concluded his diary entry:

May Heaven make it to Dei and his Maggie A VERY BRIGHT RED-LETTER DAY.

But the young couple who were being married were much too well known and popular in Criccieth for the town to allow the marriage to take place unnoticed as a hole-in-the-corner affair, and the town was decorated with flags, illuminated especially that night and bonfires lit with a firework display on the Dinas rock near the Castle. They themselves spent a ten-day honeymoon in London, and Lloyd George was involved, much to Margaret's distress, in a fracas with a cabman just as they were about to set out on the return journey. After returning to Criccieth they went to live with Margaret's parents at Mynydd Ednyfed, which was to be their home for the next three years.

CHAPTER EIGHT

PARLIAMENT

The year 1888 had opened well for Lloyd George. He had not only married the girl of his choice but had also won over her parents. He described his reception on arrival at Mynydd Ednyfed:

1888
3 Feb. Mrs. Owen very pleased to see us. Felt very awkward this first night at Mynydd Ednyfed. Both Mr. and Mrs. O. were however very kind and assisted us to feel as homely as possible.

4 Feb. In all morning—In afternoon with Mag. for tea to Morvin House. Some splendid presents have arrived both at Mynydd Ednyfed and at Morvin House, W.G. has given me exceptionally handsome present—astounded me.

William George had been working in the Porthmadog office on his brother's wedding day, and Lloyd George realized that with such a devoted brother to run the legal practice his bridge into the future rested on a firm foundation. Lloyd George was realist enough to know that more than devotion was required on the part of his younger brother if he were to be free to follow his political career. He needed a brother who was capable, both physically and mentally, of running the practice virtually single-handed for long periods at a time; and who, moreover, would at the same time allow him to draw on the profits. Time alone would show how long his luck would hold, but no one could on the initial evidence have had a more encouraging start than Lloyd George. Margaret's loyalty to him had already been tested and had triumphed over parental and sectarian prejudice.

The conditions for constructing his bridge into the future from the Welsh bank of the river were also just right in 1888. Following Michael Davitt's speech at Blaenau Ffestiniog in February 1886, Lloyd George had become Secretary of the Anti-Tithe League for South Caernarfonshire. The opposition among farmers to the payment of tithe had been gathering momentum gradually for about fifty years, since the Tithe Commutation Act 1836. By the 1880s the effect of the agitation in Ireland had given a much keener edge to the sense of injustice amongst Welsh tenant-farmers, and the tide of popular feeling was already beginning to flow strongly in favour of radical measures of land reform when Lloyd George became actively involved with the campaign. The abolition of tithe was only one of the campaign's objectives. The others were a Land Act providing for fair rents, security of agricultural tenure and compensation for improvements effected by the tenant; the abolition of the Gaming Laws; reform of the House of Lords and the disestablishment and disendowment of the Church of England in Wales.

Unofficial surveys carried out revealed that 229,640 more people frequented nonconformist chapels than the Anglican churches in North Wales and 379,684 in South Wales. In 1886 some farmers in the Vale of Clwyd refused to pay their tithe and incidents occurred when distraint was levied on their stock. The unrest continued throughout 1887, and in February 1888 thirty-two men were prosecuted at Ruthin Assizes for riotous assembly. The strength of popular feeling in their favour, however, was so great that the authorities were afraid of the consequences of the defendants being convicted and punished. The prosecution at the trial offered no evidence and the case was dropped. Lloyd George had already realized that 'this tithe business is an excellent lever wherewith to raise the spirit of the people.'* T. E. Ellis, the member for Merioneth, took over the leadership of the older group of Liberal M.Ps. in the House of Commons, and moved that Wales should have its own Act to reform the system of land tenure and related problems. The cry was to give the land back to the people.

The veteran leader of the anti-tithe and land reform movement was Thomas Gee of Denbigh, the founder of the Welsh radical newspaper *Y Faner*. Lloyd George, as secretary of the movement in South Caernarfonshire, arranged for Thomas Gee to address meetings in the area in May 1888, and made sure that Gee and himself as the principal supporting speaker should receive the maximum publicity by engaging the Criccieth Town crier to go around on Fair Day to announce the meetings. For this Richard Lloyd paid the crier the princely sum of one shilling. Considerable local interest was aroused by Gee's visit, inasmuch as he had been openly criticizing Ellis-Nanney of Llanystumdwy for his action in serving David Evans, the tenant of a Merioneth farm which he owned with a notice to quit. Evans was taking a leading part in the anti-tithe campaign, and Nanney's agent, Walter B. C. Jones of Criccieth, had written to him:

---

* Lloyd George to T. E. Ellis, 19 May 1887 (National Library of Wales, Ellis Papers, 679).

It is quite impossible for any landowner to spend money in the face of the Welsh Land League started by Mr. Gee of Denbigh. You will have received the new agreement and if you will consider it carefully, and with an unbiased mind, you will say it is fair. . . . Tenants will have to choose whom they will have as their friends—their landlords or the Welsh Land League.

Yours truly,

WALTER B. C. JONES

David Evans declined to sign the new agreement and accordingly received notice to quit. When Gee visited Criccieth Nanney came in for a lot of hostile criticism for victimizing his Merioneth tenant. Lloyd George did not know then that he would be contesting the Caernarfon Boroughs constituency against Ellis-Nanney in a bye-election within less than two years, but he knew that Nanney's tactical error in serving his tenant with a notice to quit would help the cause of Welsh radicalism. Up to that time Ellis-Nanney had kept his copy-book as a landlord relatively clean. In political terms, with Lloyd George hotly in pursuit of the constituency's nomination as Liberal candidate, this error was a bonus for Lloyd George. He cited W. B. C. Jones's letter, and claimed with great effect that he was the tenants' friend in south Caernarfonshire.

The event, however, which made Lloyd George the firm favourite for the nomination was the Llanfrothen burial case which came before Judge Bishop at the Porthmadog County Court in May 1888. This case, which fell like a ripe plum into the lap of the newly founded firm of Lloyd George & George, was an extraordinary stroke of good fortune. It revived a nonconformist grievance which the law of the land had remedied eight years earlier. The Burials Act 1880 had given nonconformists the right to bury their dead in parish churchyards in accordance with their own forms of service, conducted by nonconformist ministers. In 1888 no one would have expected a parish rector to be so foolish as to deny this right to a nonconformist family in Llanfrothen, but this is exactly what the Reverend Richard Jones, Rector of Llanfrothen since 1870, did in April 1888, when he was served with a notice by Evan Roberts under the 1880 Act that he wished to have his brother buried in a recently enclosed addition to the old churchyard. The rector did not like the Act and attempted to reserve from its operation this addition by getting the donor to attach to the Deed of Gift, made in 1881, a condition that only burials conducted in accordance with the rites of the established Church could be made therein.

Initially the rector assumed that the Roberts family would agree to the service being conducted by him so that the deceased could be buried alongside his daughter, who was already buried in this addition to the old churchyard; accordingly a grave was opened and partially dug when the notice under the Act was served. The rector then ordered the partially excavated grave to be filled up, and the deceased's brother and son took legal advice at the Porthmadog office of Lloyd George & George. They were advised to go ahead with their intention of burying the deceased in the new portion, and his brother, son and their helpers reopened the grave in readiness for the funeral on 27 April. On that day some of the relatives, finding the gate of the cemetery locked, went to the rectory and asked the rector for the key to the churchyard. When it was refused, again acting on Lloyd George's advice, they broke open the gate with a crowbar, and, obtaining the loan of a bier from a neighbouring chapel, took the body into the churchyard and interred it in the new portion, a Methodist minister conducting the burial service.

These events had already attracted a considerable amount of publicity, but if the rector had realized the error of his ways and accepted defeat with good grace, the case would not have assumed the importance it did in the Lloyd George story. What he did was to consult Hugh Vincent of Bangor, a prominent solicitor and churchman, who must have advised him that he had a good case in trespass against the Roberts family and their helpers. This was the case which came before Judge Bishop the following month. Lloyd George had already recorded that Judge Bishop was prejudiced against him and that he wished a more fair-minded and liberal judge had been appointed. The rector would not have stood a chance of success, in view of the provisions of the 1880 Act, before an unprejudiced judge who would have regarded the rector as a cleric who was still living under the old pre-1880 dispensation and had been unable to change his attitude to accord with the law of the land. The facts in relation to the alleged trespass were not in dispute, and at the opening of the case Lloyd George accepted the version of what had occurred as related by Vincent. There were, however, two issues of fact to be decided: firstly, whether the piece of land verbally gifted by the donor in 1864 was an addition to the old churchyard, and, secondly, whether or not it had been occupied as such by the rector and the parishioners so as to have excluded the donor from possession for a period of over twelve years. If the answer to the second question was in the affirmative, then that was an end of the rector's case, because in 1881 the donor would be purporting to attach a condition to the conveyance of a plot of land of which the donor was no longer the owner. These two issues of fact were crucial to the case, and Lloyd George was not prepared to entrust the decision to Bishop, so he requisitioned a jury. At the conclusion of the evidence Bishop summed up, and left, as he was bound to, these questions of fact for their decision. The foreman read out the jury's decision:

We all agree there was a verbal gift in 1864 of the addition to the old Churchyard and was actually occupied by the Rector and parishioners ever since.

William George was present in Court throughout the hearing and took down a shorthand note of the evidence and the jury's verdict. The foreman, after reading the verdict, handed the slip of paper it was written on to the judge who adjourned the case for two months and said he would then hear legal argument. William George worked assiduously on the case, and his notes and comments are with the original papers in my possession. At the resumed hearing it soon became apparent that the judge in his own note had wrongly recorded the jury's verdict, and armed with his brother's shorthand note, Lloyd George demanded that the judge should amend and correct his own erroneous record of the jury's verdict. The judge refused to do so, unless Vincent agreed; he refused in turn, and William George for the use of the Court of Appeal made an affidavit, to which was exhibited his transcribed shorthand note of the proceedings, including the reserved judgement awarding the rector nominal damages for trespass with the costs of the action. The appeal came on for hearing five months later* and the Lord Chief Justice sitting with another judge allowed the appeal, after checking the jury's verdict as recorded on the foreman's note. The Court clearly disapproved of the rector's conduct, the Lord Chief Justice stating:

People may persuade themselves that they are doing in the name of religion what they would be very much ashamed to do in any other name. The simple question of fact is—Has the donor been out of possession since 1864? The Jury have found that she has. Every circumstance of the case shows that she has. The jury were perfectly right in finding that she has and if she has, there is an end of the Plaintiff's claim. . . . The County Court Judge was wrong and his verdict must be reversed.

Not only did Lloyd George & George win this appeal but they succeeded in drawing the Court of Appeal's attention to the

* 15 December 1888.

conduct of the County Court judge, the Lord Chief Justice directing:

A part of the conduct of the County Court Judge will be submitted to a superior Master—the Lord Chancellor. I have nothing to do with his conduct in that respect, that is for the Lord Chancellor.

The Llanfrothen case did not establish any new principle of law, and its historical importance lies in the decisive boost it gave Lloyd George in his sustained effort to be adopted as Liberal candidate for the Caernarfon Boroughs constituency. It was interpreted as a triumph for nonconformists against the oppression of the established Church, and for the cause of the tenant-farmer and quarryman against the rule of the privileged minority. The verdict could not have come at a more favourable time from Lloyd George's point of view—a fortnight before the meeting of the Caernarfon Boroughs Liberal Association. The last item on the agenda for this meeting was the selection of a candidate.

The Caernarfon Boroughs—a constituency which vanished a few years after Lloyd George's death in 1945—consisted of the ancient boroughs of the county of Caernarfon, extending from Criccieth and Nefyn in the south of the county to Conwy, which included the rapidly developing town of Llandudno, in the north of the county. The borough of Caernarfon itself lay at the heart of the constituency, which lacked territorial cohesion, the various boroughs being separated from each other by vast tracts of agricultural land and more recently established towns, such as Porthmadog. Lloyd George's first objective was to gain the support of the local associations in each of the boroughs, and he made a systematic survey of the key men in each. His first task was to win over the associations of Criccieth, Pwllheli and Nefyn; this was accomplished by the middle of the summer of 1888. He then turned his attention to Caernarfon and concentrated his efforts in raising support in the town and surrounding district for starting a Liberal club in the town. The sitting member for the Caernarfon Boroughs was Edmund Swetenham, Q.C., a Conservative. Lloyd George realized that the town's Conservative club with the social opportunities it afforded was a focal point of the Conservative party's strength in the borough. He spoke in several of the villages outside Caernarfon itself in support of the Liberal club, and was well received. At one of these meetings in July 1888 the chairman referred to him as '*Un o sêr y dyfodol*' (One of the stars of the future). He often left Criccieth at week-ends to attend meetings such as this, and contrived to have a meeting in the chapel on the Sunday morning, when he gave an address on Temperance, as a follow-up to the political meeting on the Saturday night. Uncle Lloyd, disapproving of David's absence on this account from the Sunday services at Criccieth, commented in his diary: 'Don't believe in his Saturday and Sunday off policy.'

Lloyd George knew that he had an uphill task and could not afford to allow any stone to be left unturned if he were to succeed in his objective. His rivals for the candidature were a nonconformist minister and a professor from Trinity College, Dublin. He mentions in his diary a Liberal meeting which was held during June 1888 in Caernarfon itself; at that time it would appear that T. E. Ellis's friend, D. R. Daniel, was under consideration also:

Liberal meeting at C'fon. Daniel and others speaking in same meeting. So far as speaking was concerned I believe and am told that I licked Daniel and the whole lot. . . . Believe that I have made my mark at C'fon and that I will stand a very good chance, when the time comes to select a candidate, to get a very respectable no. of partisans in C'fon.

The selection meeting was called for a date in October 1888. In September he had still not won over the Bangor Association; and on 5 September he wrote to the Secretary to complain that the fifteen minutes allocated to him for speaking was not sufficient for him to place his political views adequately before the delegates. He wanted to know what time was being allowed to the other candidates. A few days after this he noticed in the local press that Mr. William Jones, a pork butcher of Bangor and a leading member of the Bangor association, had made a strong speech in support of the Temperance cause. Lloyd George never missed an opportunity to further his candidature by flattery, so he wrote to Mr. Jones, a complete stranger to him:

Private   Criccieth.
                                                                                          18 Sept. 1888.
My dear friend,
Many hearty congratulations to you and your colleagues upon the truly glorious triumph you scored last week. Had the temperance cause such energetic fanatics in every town and village throughout Wales, I am thoroughly convinced the fiendish traffic would soon be a thing of the past. I shall be at Bangor spending Sunday with some friends. Have you any Sunday evening meetings?
                                                            Yours faithfully,
                                                            D. LLOYD GEORGE

Mr. Jones later in the month made another speech for the Temperance cause in Merioneth, and on 28 September Lloyd

F   157

George followed up his earlier letter with a further message of enthusiastic congratulations, and pointing out that: 'In a recent case before the Barmouth magistrates, I succeeded in securing the closing down of a public house at Dyffryn, a nearby village.'

When the Caernarfon Boroughs Liberal Association met in October the decision to select a candidate was postponed, in spite of Lloyd George's efforts during the months before, and he wrote the next day to his agent:

My dear Roberts,

I regret that R.D. through his minions succeeded so well in his design last night. His object was delay and he has gained it. Our plan must be to frustrate him in his ultimate aim. . . . The mess they have made of it at Caernarfon last night has, in fact, affected the other boroughs, and the work will have to be done all over again.

D. LLOYD GEORGE

After this set-back, so as to avoid giving the impression he was at every one's beck and call, he wrote to the secretaries of the various associations inviting each to give a list of dates, any one of which would be available for him to attend an association meeting. By the time he received a reply Lloyd George would find that his engagement book had filled up, and he would answer the secretary's letter invariably stating: 'Of the dates you mention only one is now available.' He also realized that women could well influence their husbands' decisions, and accordingly requested that he would like to know when 'the Ladies League Meeting is to be held in Caernarfon'. It is significant that in the letters Lloyd George wrote in support of his candidature at this period his references to land reform, the anti-tithe campaign and the need for legislation to disendow the established Church in Wales are conspicuous for their absence; invariably the lever he used to gain favour with the Liberal delegates was an avowal of his complete dedication to the cause of Temperance. In his diary* entries for January 1889 Lloyd George described how he was finally adopted:

1889

3 Jan. Selection of candidate last thing on programme so I had to wait upstairs for 2 hours. Had excellent reception. Delegates got up and cheered me. Felt position keenly. Could not speak with much verve. . . . Proposed by T. C. Lewis, who said he preferred me from the first; seconded by a Capt John Williams from Conwy, who said:

---

* This diary is with the Carey-Evans collection of the Lloyd George papers at the National Library of Wales, Aberystwyth.

'*Y mae nhw wedi'i lyncu o yng Nghonwy a Llandudno acw.*' [They have fallen for him in Conwy and Llandudno.] My father and mother-in-law appear pleased.

4 Jan. G. P. Williams [Criccieth, an old family friend] quite excited—says that when he looked at me in meeting yesterday addressing delegates as accepted Liberal candidate, he recollected the little boy from Llanystumdwy with knickerbockers and red stockings. 'A lump came into my throat,' G.P. said [in Welsh] 'and tears flowed from the corner of my eyes.'

As soon as he had been selected as the Liberal candidate for the Caernarfon Boroughs constituency Lloyd George threw himself with characteristic zest into the county council election campaign. The first elections to appoint the councillors to serve on the newly established county councils under the Local Government Act 1888 were held that January. Lloyd George decided not to stand for election himself, but toured Caernarfonshire from end to end, addressing a whole series of meetings in support of the individual Liberal candidates. Several of these had supported his adoption as parliamentary Liberal candidate, and in addition to his desire to see the Liberal cause triumph in the county he wished to repay these supporters for their loyalty to him. It was during this campaign that Lloyd George appeared on a political platform for the first time with Arthur Acland, the Liberal member for Rotherham. Acland had a house at Clynnog in Caernarfonshire and had taken a lively interest in Welsh politics for some years. He was a close friend of T. E. Ellis, and had an important influence on him and on other young Welsh radicals of that period. Acland was about fifteen years older than Lloyd George, who readily accepted his invitation to stay with him for a week-end during the county council campaign. Acland also used to invite Ellis to be his guest, and he helped bring the two together before Lloyd George joined his senior colleague in Parliament. The theme of Lloyd George's speeches during this campaign was that patriotic, Liberal-minded and democratic Welshmen should be returned throughout Wales to serve on the new county councils. In this way the movement for Welsh self-government would be advanced. This election campaign more than any other single event until then helped to arouse a feeling of national identity in Wales for the first time for centuries, and the Liberals won control of every county in Wales, including Monmouth with the exception of Brecon. Caernarfonshire County Council was composed mainly of Liberals, but it was significant that Ellis-Nanney who was to be Lloyd George's opponent in the 1890 bye-election, was returned as the member for

159

Lloyd George's home village. For their part in promoting the Liberal victory in Caernarfonshire both Acland and Lloyd George were amongst the first of the county council's aldermen. As Lloyd George was only twenty-six he became known as 'The Boy Alderman', a title which clung to him for many years.

An indication of the influence already wielded by Lloyd George in the county is contained in a letter he received from T. E. Ellis: 'Acland has been pressed to stand for the London County Council. That would mean him leaving Clynnog altogether. . . . That would be a heavy loss to us, and I should like to bind him to us by having him as Alderman of Caernarfon County Council. Please send me word *per return* whether you think it possible.'

In January 1889 there were still three more years to go before the next parliamentary General Election. With Liberalism triumphant throughout Wales, and in the county of Caernarfon in particular, an aspiring young politician in Lloyd George's position might well have rested on his laurels for a few months. Not so Lloyd George. He set about making a detailed appraisal of the state of the party organization in the Boroughs; he carefully checked the electoral registers and found them unsatisfactory. His experience as polling clerk and Liberal canvasser with Breese, Jones & Casson had given him a professional insight into this vital aspect of electioneering. A good instance of his concern to bring back into the Liberal fold a Unionist sheep that had strayed is to be found in a letter he wrote to 'Mr. Rees, Nefyn' on 23 March 1889. It is a long letter, and I will only quote a few sentences:

I certainly do not estimate your support at so insignificant a price as you seem yourself disposed to place on it. I quite agree with you that it is very unlikely that you will abandon either your Liberalism or your nonconformity. I have too high an opinion of both your shrewdness and your principle to believe you capable of that. . . . Now that Gladstone has conceded the points for which all honest Unionists fought I really cannot find a reason for you not joining the party. . . . It is a question of religious freedom and equality for our country, and the liberating from the oppression of the Landlords.

This letter shows that Lloyd George by this time had realized the threat to his political future the Gladstone-Chamberlain schism might cause within the Welsh Liberal party. In 1886, when Richard Lloyd told him that 'Chamberlain was astray', he disagreed and stood up for Chamberlain. Now that he was entrusted with responsibility he became more of a realist. At this early stage of his political career he revealed also one of those traits which distinguished him from most of his contemporaries, both as politicians and statesmen: the determination to get the best available expert advice, regardless of the quarter from which it might come, provided that the adviser was in general sympathy with his objective at the time. Lloyd George's objective in the spring of 1889 was to make the Liberal organization of the Caernarfon Boroughs as efficient as it could be by the time he anticipated he would be fighting his first parliamentary election in 1892. He knew the parable of the wise and foolish virgins by heart and was determined that he would have sufficient oil to light his lamp to lead him along his chosen political path, whenever that election might come. The secretary of the National Liberal Federation at that time was Francis Schnadhorst of Birmingham, a prominent Liberal who had remained loyal to Gladstone. He was the expert to whom Lloyd George decided to write for advice:

27th April 1889

Dear Sir,

I have been selected by the Liberal association in the Caernarfon Boroughs as their candidate to contest the seat at the next election. May I trouble you for your valuable advice upon the most efficient methods of organization so as to ensure victory?

The parties are pretty evenly balanced in the constituency. At the '85 election Sir Love Parry retained the seat for the (Liberal) party by the narrow majority of 65. At the '86 election Mr. Swetenham, the sitting member, gained the seat for the Tories by a majority of 136. The Liberal defeat was due entirely to poor organization and apathy. The Conservative organization was at that date and still is excellent.

The Liberal party suffers from lack of the necessary funds. Registration has not therefore been energetically attended to and one or two clubs have collapsed. The Tories on the other hand are plentifully supplied with cash. As to registration our weaknesses have to some extent been remedied by the efforts of volunteers, but the clubs still languish. . . .

Will you kindly furnish me with some hints regarding the organization which I might submit to the Executive Committee, especially upon the following points:

1. As to public meetings—whether they should be held throughout the Boroughs *forthwith*.

2. As to bazaars—whether they have been found to be desirable and effective for raising funds for political purposes; or do they tend to damage the Liberal cause by offending local tradesmen?

Your early reply will greatly oblige.

Yours truly,

D. LLOYD GEORGE

161

I have been unable to find Francis Schnadhorst's reply, but judging from the number of letters Lloyd George wrote in May to the various officials connected with the electoral registers, I gather he was advised to redouble his efforts in this direction. Undoubtedly he owed his victory by the narrow margin of eighteen votes (after a recount) in the 1890 bye-election to the detailed work he and William put into revising these registers and insisting on having them brought up to date.

The office copy-letter books from the date of Lloyd George's adoption onwards show that he became increasingly involved with his political interests. Not a week passed without him writing several letters to further the programme he considered Welsh Liberals should adopt, and these letters were addressed to some key figures who later became the leaders of the Cymru Fydd (Young Wales) movement. One of the most regular of his correspondents at that time on both political and legal matters was Ellis Jones Griffith, who had been called to the Bar in 1887 after being President of the Cambridge Union and obtaining a first in the Law Tripos. Although Griffith was three years older and Lloyd George had not even had a secondary education, he wrote to Griffith with as much self-assurance as if he himself had been President of the Union. The following is an extract from one of his letters:

28 May, 1889

My dear Griffith,

Here are the instructions in the Right of Way case. I hope to send you a nice of breach of promise in a few days. The drafting of a statement of claim in such a case is much more delightful than in a right of way action.

Wales is thoroughly disgusted with old Gladstone. I think we ought to say so in pretty plain language through the medium of resolutions in public meetings. What is the Welsh parliamentary party doing? And what does it propose doing? It figured very wretchedly in the recent disestablishment debate. Not one speech of any note. Why didn't Ellis speak? I am glad that Dillwyn raised the question of Welsh Home Rule. . . .

L. Llewelyn Dillwyn was the Liberal member for Swansea and had supported the movement for the disestablishment of the Church in Wales from the beginning in 1870. In Parliament he had spoken up for the tenants who had been evicted from their farms following the 1868 election. He was a prominent Radical, and in 1887 he had come out strongly in favour of Irish self-government. He was a banker and had taken a leading part in the industrial development of Swansea. Lloyd George had felt for some time that the movement for land reform needed to be raised and enlarged to embrace not only agrarian reforms but also the removal of social injustice in the industrial areas. He saw in the veteran Dillwyn a Welsh politican who had a vision of Wales as one nation, but he was disappointed by the showing of the other Welsh members in the debate in the House of Commons in May 1889 on Dillwyn's motion calling for the disestablishment of the Church in Wales. In a letter to a Liberal client commenting on this debate, he said:

Very disappointing. Our servility has induced the G.O.M. [Gladstone] to believe he can ignore us to any extent.

The clearest exposition of Lloyd George's vision of the need to deal politically with *all* the issues affecting Wales, and not merely the agrarian grievances, is contained in a letter he wrote to Howel Gee of Denbigh, a son of Thomas Gee, Chairman of the Welsh Land League. On his father's behalf Howel Gee had sent Lloyd George a copy of the draft constitution of the Welsh Land League, inviting his comments:

7 November 1887

Dear Friend,

The land question seems to have been presented as a matter affecting *farmers only*, whereas there are other classes quite as vitally affected. For instance;

(a) *Agricultural labourers*. Inexplicable omission. Here is a class more numerous and far more fearless than our cautious Welsh farmers. The Government's allotment scheme is a sham and a delusion; falls far short of Chamberlain's scheme which was a really great idea.

(b) *Building Leases*. Another glaring omission. We ought to add the fixing of fair ground rents and the enfranchisement of leaseholds upon that basis; and I shall tell you why—the Conservatives seem to have a stronger hold upon the town than the counties.

(c) Land question as it affects *mining interests* is completely ignored. This will lose the support of miners & quarrymen, people engaged in the iron industries in Wales of all classes. Their grievance is quite as acute as any of the farmers.

The prosperity of Wales depends quite as much if not more upon reasonable mining leases as upon agrarian reform. English capital would flow in were not forfeiture clauses so prohibitory.

(d) If you mean to make the League a really *national* one you must include in its *programme all* classes of the nation, who suffer the wrongs of our infamous agrarian system.

Mind you, I would not for a moment belittle the farmer. I am a

163

farmer's son—grandson & great grandson & so on since times 'wherein the memory of man runneth not to the contrary', but what I am urging is this: that the movement ought to be a thoroughly national one, and that the farmers should not be left to bear the whole brunt of the struggle themselves.

Yours very truly,

D. LLOYD GEORGE

Although several leading Welsh politicians of the period were lawyers, Lloyd George had no intention of settling down to the quiet round of a country solicitor's practice, appearing in court on routine cases, addressing the bench of magistrates with deference and accepting their adverse verdicts with good grace. In May 1889 four quarrymen were charged before the Caernarfon Magistrates Court with unlawfully netting trout in the Nantlle lower lake. Lloyd George appeared on their behalf, and claimed that a public right to fish this lake had been established since time immemorial. The chairman of the magistrates said that would have to be proved in a higher court.

The newspaper report records the sequel to this comment:

Mr. George: Yes, sir, and in a perfectly unbiased Court too.

The Chairman: If that remark of Mr. George's is meant as a reflection upon a magistrate sitting on this Bench, I hope that he will name him. A more insulting and ungentlemanly remark to the Bench I have never heard during the course of my experience as a magistrate.

Mr. George: But a more true remark was never made in a Court of Justice.

The Chairman: Tell me to whom you are referring.

Mr. George: I refer to you in particular, sir.

The Chairman: Then I retire from the Chair. Good-bye, gentlemen. This is the first time I have ever been insulted in a Court of Justice.

The remaining magistrates then requested Lloyd George to apologize before he proceeded with the case, but he refused to do so, and they eventually decided to hear the remainder of the evidence. There was no substance in law to the defence, but Lloyd George's self-assurance and uncompromising boldness in the conduct of the case made him into something of a folk-hero amongst the quarrymen of the Nantlle valley. An attack upon the magistracy was unheard of and several magistrates wrote to him asking him to justify or withdraw his remarks. This is part of a letter he wrote in reply to one magistrate:

You invite my opinion as to your demeanour at the Court. I must honestly say that it was such as led me to believe that you were more intent on protecting the fish in the Nentlle lakes against the inroads of quarrymen, than in doing justice in that particular case according to the evidence.

This bravado was, of course, all very well in the case of some one who did not anticipate having to appear regularly before the Caernarfon magistrates. William George was more concerned; cases such as this were to be no springboard for him into the political arena. William George had all along advised him to temper down his attacks on the magistracy, 'or that club of aristocracy or the J.P.-dom as D. calls it. He will lose a great deal more than he will gain by putting himself in a position of personal antagonism with the bench.' William was also worried because his brother had no time for the routine cases: 'He is getting disgusted with these petty cases.'

Lloyd George did not confine his efforts to improve the efficiency of the Liberals to the Caernarfon Boroughs. Having persuaded his brother to take an active interest in improving the efficiency of the local Liberal party, he then started writing to various solicitors asking them to join the Executive of the North Wales Liberal Federation. Most consented to do so, although reluctantly. A Caernarfon solicitor, R. Arthur Griffith, said of the Federation: 'This much is certain—it is a failure; but what can be done? It won't do to attack the old slugs without some alternative policy.' When he received an official invitation to second a resolution on the disestablishment of the Church at a meeting of the North Wales Federation in October 1889, Lloyd George turned the invitation down and said he would instead speak on the last motion on the agenda relating to the organization of the Liberal party throughout Wales. He added:

Unless we have a more thorough and active system of organization than we now possess, we cannot succeed but very imperfectly in our national aims. It is not a matter of securing a nominal measure of disestablishment and disendowment, nor must it be a measure of the description of the one which was conceded to Ireland. . . . We must make certain of a real measure of disendowment and not a sham. We must also organize the people of Wales—so that when the time comes for settling this question we can speak confidently in their name.

Lloyd George asked R. Arthur Griffith to propose that 'the Welsh National Council [of Liberals] and the Welsh Liberal Federations should be converted into one organization to be called the Welsh National League'. In seconding this resolution, which he had clearly inspired, Lloyd George spoke at great length. He

165

deplored the 'historical blunder of our forefathers, which conduced to the loss of our national independence, occasioned by the division of Wales into the two provinces of North and South'. He laid particular emphasis on the importance of the Liberals throughout the country having an organization which could protect 'every working man who happens to be subjected to the persecution of a Tory employer of labour. . . . Liberalism could then be the ruling force in the country.' The theme of his speech was openly critical of the Welsh Liberal leaders, and bearing in mind that the Liberals had just scored such outstanding successes in the county council elections throughout Wales and held twenty-eight of the thirty-four parliamentary seats, it is not surprising that some of them regarded his criticism as unjustified effrontery on his part. The motion was lost.

The South Wales Liberal Federation marched in advance of its North Wales counterpart, and at a meeting of the South Wales Federation in February 1890 a resolution was proposed favouring self-government for Wales 'in purely domestic affairs'; Lloyd George made a powerful speech in seconding the resolution, arguing effectively that the arguments advanced in support of granting self-government to Ireland applied in every instance with equal, if not greater, relevance to Wales. The difference between the Welsh and the Irish was that the Welsh possessed greater patience:

We have never quarrelled with tyranny as the Irish have done. We have rather turned the other cheek to the smiter. . . . This resolution is a fitting climax to this meeting's programme. You have pledged yourselves to—Disestablishment, Land Reform, Local Option and other great reforms. *But, however drastic and broad they may appear to be, they after all simply touch the fringe of that vast social question which must be dealt with in the near future. There is a momentous time coming. The dark continent of wrong is being explored and there is a missionary spirit abroad for its reclamation to the realm of right.* . . . That is why I feel so sanguine that were self-government granted to Wales she would be a model to the nationalities of the earth of a people who have driven oppression from their hillsides, and initiated the glorious reign of freedom, justice and truth.

The words I have italicized in the above extract from his speech indicate that his political concern and vision extended beyond granting self-government to Wales. He may not have explained what he meant by the 'vast social question' to which he referred, but his recorded diary entries and memoranda, and the books he had read make it plain that his vision was of a Wales in which brotherhood and social justice would reign supreme, and provide an inspiration and example for other countries. The roots of this social concern were embedded in the soil of his native Caernarfonshire, in the deprivations which his family and himself had suffered and were still enduring. Throughout his life his main ambition was to make himself into a first-class fighting politician to remove the conditions which perpetuated social injustices and class-privilege from generation to generation, and also to fashion the Liberal party into an efficient instrument to initiate the necessary reforms and get them adopted constitutionally by Parliament.

He was a constitutional rebel in that he aimed to overthrow the existing social order and replace it with a more egalitarian social structure, by constitutional means. He was a natural democrat, in that he believed in the efficacy of the public media of expression— the press and the platform speech in his day—to gain the support of the majority.

When he made this speech in February Lloyd George could not have foreseen that within a month he would be contesting a bye-election in the Caernarfon Boroughs. This was brought about by the death of the Conservative member, Edmund Swetenham, in March. One of the first to write a letter to Lloyd George wishing him well was John Parry, the Denbighshire anti-tithe campaign leader. He saw the death of Swetenham as the dawn of a new era. He wrote (21 March 1890):

Dear Friend,
The death of Edmund Swetenham is rejoicingly announced about here. Now is your opportunity.

Inevitably, William George, already hard-pressed by Lloyd George's continual absences from the office on political matters, viewed the situation with mixed feelings. He recorded in his diary:

1890
24 March 'It never rains but it pours!' Just as I was emerging from one excitement and fondly promising myself a period of fishing and recreation, by George, here we are plunged right in the midst of another whirlpool of excitement by the cry—'Swetenham is dead!' I plainly heard the cry as I was dropping on the (Criccieth) platform. Since then a perpetual contest has gone on in my little world between the force of new circumstances and the power of routine. David is knocking backwards and forwards a good deal between here and Caernarfon. Everything goes on swimmingly to all appearances. I was up with him last night (Sunday night!) concocting the address. I think we have succeeded in making a good and stirring one in the end.

T. E. Ellis, the young Welsh politician who shared Lloyd George's vision of a self-governing Wales and one Welsh Liberal party was unfortunately in Egypt trying to recover his health at this time. He would have been a great help to Lloyd George in the bye-election contest. He wrote him a long letter regretting Swetenham's death on personal grounds and adding:

As I looked across the floor of the House of Commons on his kind face, I wondered a thousand times how in the world he had been elected to represent my countrymen in the Caernarvon Boroughs. For it was one of the chief principles of his policy that Wales ought not to expect to obtain any special legislation, and that to merge herself and her national identity in the life of England and Anglicanism was her duty and her only salvation. You take a very different view of the future of Wales as regards politics and national life. . . .

Ellis Griffith, the barrister with whom Lloyd George had had many business and social contacts by this time, wrote to him:

The struggle has come earlier than we thought. I do hope that all will rally to the cause, and pardon me, if I suggest, that you must be as conciliatory as possible. . . . Of course, nothing will be done until after the funeral & pray don't give the others an excuse for saying you have not observed this etiquette. . . . Be careful about the address. The seat must be won.

Lloyd George was warned by supporters from various parts of the constituency that the contest would be a close one, and that he must not 'leave a stone unturned' if he were to succeed in capturing the seat for the Liberals. In his election address Lloyd George conceded that 'the wrongs of Ireland must of necessity have the first claim upon the attention of the Liberal party'. This appeared to be a considerable modification of the views he had expressed in his South Wales speech, in which he laid emphasis on Wales's right to have a government of her own; in his election address self-government is not specifically mentioned. 'First and foremost stands the cause of religious liberty and equality in Wales,' he said in the address, which was pitched in such a low key, that a prominent Bangor supporter, Morgan Richards, wrote to him:

On carefully reading your address to-day, with a view to moving a vote of confidence in you at our meeting to-night, I was sorry and greatly disappointed to find that you in it truckle to party and electioneering exigencies and make *expediency* the measure of your political faith! You have been bidding for the last two or three years for political popularity by dangling before the constituency Home Rule

168

for Wales and nationalization of the land. In vain do I look for the
mention of these great subjects in your common-phrased-stereotyped
address. I presume you have quietly dropped them to conciliate the
'moderates' whom you have always denounced.

One of the most influential nonconformist leaders in nineteenth-
century Wales, the veteran Dr. John Thomas, wrote to Lloyd
George offering his support during the campaign, and warned him:

I know it will be a hard fight; and a desperate fight. I am afraid of
some of our most moderate men, that they will not take a bold line and
make your advanced views their excuse. I must say that I cannot go so
far as you go on what is termed Home Rule for Wales; and I am
afraid that the prominence given to this question may do us harm in
some places; and especially in the Boroughs. Our great question in
Wales is disestablishment. I care little for the question of Home rule,
even for Ireland compared to this question. You are quite safe with
the advance party. The danger is with the moderates, as they wish to
be called, and we cannot carry the Caernarvon Boroughs without
them.

Lloyd George knew that John Thomas was right on the importance of gaining the support of the moderates, and William
George believed that some Tory voters would also need to be won
over to be sure of victory. William George threw himself into the
campaign, canvassing on his brother's behalf throughout the constituency and sent him detailed reports. The result of a full day's
canvass at Conwy confirmed that the 'great subject to dwell upon
is Disestablishment'.

In his diary entry for Easter Monday, 7 April, William George
provides us with an insight into the progress of the campaign:

We are in the thick of the fight. Personal rather than party feeling runs
high. The Tories began by ridiculing D.'s candidature; they have
now changed their tune. Each party looks upon it as a stiff fight. . . .
The Tories are in the first place anxious to retain the seat for the sake
of their prestige; but above their zeal for party prestige their zeal for
their class prestige over-tops all. The struggle is not so much a struggle
of Tory v. Liberal or Radical even; the main issue is between county
squire and the upstart democrat. The cry given by this issue unites
the Tories and I am afraid tends to disunite the Liberals—all the
snobs are not outside the walls of Liberalism. This will no doubt tell
against D to a certain extent, but I am hoping that the integrating
forces are stronger than those of disintegration.

Richard Lloyd gives an account in his diary of the election day,

10 April 1890, and of the following day when the count took place at Caernarfon:

W.G. at polling booth here. All polled to the man—a new thing in our borough-town history. Been to Afonwen to see Dei—he looked extraordinarily well, not sanguine at all. Watkin [a local squire] refused to swear W.G.'s declaration of secrecy. Revenge openly admitted! !

Lloyd George won the election (after a recount) by a majority of 18—1,963 votes to 1,945.

11 April W.G. at counting Caernarfon. D.Ll.G to Pwllheli, met him at Afonwen. Received 24 telegrams to congratulate D. on his victory—Almost a miracle—The greatest crowd of people ever witnessed in this place on any similar occasion—Wild with enthusiasm, though some tried to throw wet blanket on my show—But the people's cause will have to be emphasized by the people's warmth of heart against all contra protestations and influences.

After the result had been announced in Caernarfon the excitement was tremendous, and the newly elected member was hailed by his enthusiastic supporters when he appeared on the balcony of the Guildhall after the declaration of the poll. They then dragged his carriage through the crowded streets of the county town. He was given an equally enthusiastic welcome at Pwllheli, and at Criccieth bonfires were lit in his honour on the night of the 11th. Following the celebration of his victory at Criccieth, Lloyd George rested at his wife's parents' home at Mynydd Ednyfed, before leaving for London on 16 April to take his seat in Parliament the following day. On the way to London, at Conwy station, he was met by hundreds of cheering supporters. He decided to break his journey before continuing to London by a later train. His friends were delighted and drew his carriage to the Market Hall, where he addressed the meeting first in Welsh and afterwards in English. The borough of Conwy had been specially illuminated for the occasion, and when he left in the evening tumultuous cheering sped him on his way to Westminster.

The first letter he wrote on Thursday evening, 17 April, after he had taken his oath and seat in the House, was to his brother William:

My dear W.

After a very enthusiastic reception by the Liberal members of the House on my introduction by Ackland and Stuart Rendel (Mabon was not in the House) I am off to dine with my friend Sir John Puleston! !
[Puleston, a prominent Churchman, was Conservative member for

Devonport, 1874–92. At the 1892 General Election he was selected to oppose Lloyd George in the Caernarfon Boroughs. He failed to regain the seat. He was a colourful character, who had taken part in the American Civil war, and a warm-hearted supporter of Welsh causes both in London and Caernarfon.]

Goschen has just sat down, I believe, after delivering a very long speech in introducing his Budget; he has taken 2d off tea—that's one good thing. I shall write more fully to you later on. . . . *Cofia ysgrifennu at dy frawd yfory.* [Remember to write to thy brother to-morrow.]

Mewn brys gwyllt, dy frawd D.
[In a wild hurry, thy brother D.]

The reference to Mabon in this, his first letter written from London as a Member of Parliament is significant. He had hoped that Mabon would have been one of his sponsors. Mabon was the first President of the South Wales Miners' Federation and a Liberal Member of Parliament on the radical wing of the party. Lloyd George had met him on several occasions on his visits to South Wales, and they had been in correspondence with each other. The fact is that when he was elected to Parliament Lloyd George had already gained a national reputation in Wales, and shown that he was concerned with the industrial problems of South Wales as well as those uppermost in the minds of his own constituents in the Caernarfon Boroughs.

Meanwhile, with the excitement of the election gradually sub-siding, William had begun to reflect on its practical implications:

1890

16 April Whilst I am writing this D is not far from Crewe on his way to London to take his seat in Parliament to-morrow night. It is only now & again that I realize what it all means; to be elected a member of the historic English Parliament is undoubtedly a great honour and privilege; for the village lad to have beaten the parish county squire is a greater honour still. That is the bright side of the question, but there is a seamy side, and truth to tell that is the side which has been weighing most on my mind to-day. Two practical questions present themselves:

(a) How is D to live there? (b) How am I to live down here? As for D he says he will speak to Harvey Clifton [a London solicitor] in town to-morrow, and maybe they will arrange a partnership there. As for me, all I can do is to continue to work as hard as I have hitherto had the privilege of doing and let things take their course. One thing I know is certain—I am now in circumstances in which trust in Provi-dence is pre-eminently called for.

One reason the Conservatives had had for their confidence that they would retain the seat was the return to their ranks of prominent local landlords, such as the Hon. Frederick Wynn, who had at the 1880 General Election openly supported the Liberal candidate, saying that he hoped a Liberal victory would put 'the extinguisher on Nanney'. Lloyd George had had very little support from prominent Liberal politicians during the campaign; Ellis Griffith spoke at two or three meetings at the start of the electoral battle but left to join T. E. Ellis in Egypt a week or so before polling day, so he missed all the crucial eve-of-the-poll meetings. Lloyd George had to tone down his radical views severely, particularly on the issue of self-government, to stand the slightest chance of victory. It was well known, however, where he stood on this and other matters which were compelling the Welsh Liberal party of 1890 to adopt a different image from that by which the party had been known in the past.

T. E. Ellis and Ellis Griffith both wrote letters to Lloyd George immediately they had heard of his success. Tom Ellis said:

My dear George,
You have done remarkably well, and I most heartily congratulate you. Toryism had everything in its favour against you, and yet you have *won* a seat. . . . Your little speech after the declaration of the poll was excellent—it summarized the meaning of the victory—no co-ercion and freedom for Wales.

I wish I were in the House to-day to welcome you. It is comforting to look forward to getting back to the House, changed as it is by the presence there of S. T. Evans* and yourself. The real work to be done first is to thoroughly master the Tithe Bill and prepare to fight it line by line. . . . A good sturdy fight on the Tithe Bill will prepare Wales for the land struggle, which will be brought immensely nearer if the Tithe Bill gets through.

Well, dear George, my best and sincerest wishes for your success in your new career. It has many pitfalls and many responsibilities, but also not a few opportunities for promoting the good cause of Wales. *Cofion caredicaf* [Kindest regards],

THOMAS E. ELLIS

In one of his first letters to his brother from London Lloyd George asked him to let him know when the County Court was

---

* S. T. Evans, lawyer; the Liberal M.P. for Central Glamorgan. Subsequently President of the Probate, Divorce and Admiralty Division.

and what cases would be coming up: 'It wouldn't do to come down for merely paltry, trumpery cases. It would lower the firm,—eh, brother?' William George on receipt of this letter recorded in his diary: 'It is well that there are some like him and some also who are willing to do the drudgery like myself; but drudgery or not let me do it honestly and well.' Foreseeing the financial burden which would fall on William to maintain not only his widowed mother, his uncle and sister but also Lloyd George during the months he was away in London, the two brothers discussed the possibility of Lloyd George entering into a partnership with the firm's London agent, Harvey Clifton, who later became a close personal friend of William's. Clifton wrote to William concerning this proposal before he met Lloyd George to discuss the matter. William replied: 'Speaking *entre nous* I may tell you that my brother is a capital fellow for introducing business. The supplement he wants is some one that will look after it when introduced, and this, I believe, you would do.' Not surprisingly nothing came of the partnership idea with Harvey Clifton! The result was that for many years both brothers and their respective families depended on the revenue derived from the Porthmadog firm of Lloyd George & George, which, after Lloyd George's election to Parliament, was run almost wholly by William George and the local staff at Porthmadog. Richard Lloyd kept a daily record of the comings and goings of both brothers, and the load of responsibility carried by William George can be gauged from the fact that between the April 1890 bye-election and the following August Lloyd George only attended the Porthmadog office once.

Knowing the financial position as she did, and the mother already of their first-born, Richard, and expecting the birth of their second child at the end of July or early August, it was not surprising that Margaret Lloyd George was reluctant to join him in London. Nevertheless he constantly kept pressing her to join him, and she did so for weeks at a time at the various lodgings he had during these early years. An indication of the situation is afforded by an 1890 (undated) letter Margaret sent William George. This letter also shows Margaret's understanding of William's position:

Dear Frater,
Dei got your letter this morning in his new lodgings. . . . Dei wished me to ask you to send him £5 by return please. He has been using some of my money. If he doesn't get it your dear sister can't return home on Saturday without leaving her husband quite penniless in this great city. . . . He also wants you to send him a few blank cheques.

173

For goodness sake don't send him many. They are such easy things to fill in and then the slashing signature of D. Lloyd George put to them —which I fear you would not be too glad to see. He wants to pay his subscription to the Liberal Club etc., etc.

Your loving sister,
MAGGIE.

William George sent the blank cheques, and these were acknowledged by Margaret who wrote: 'D. has taken all the money you gave me. It is not I who spends the cash.'

Throughout the 1890s and until his appointment as President of the Board of Trade in 1905 Lloyd George had to depend almost entirely on the drawings he made from the firm. He was conscious that it was manifestly unjust that he left his brother to do the legal work of running the practice whilst he spent his time in London and elsewhere on his political activities, for which he received no remuneration. In these circumstances he dreamt of ways by which he could gain financial independence: the first and most recurrent idea, which was put into practice for a time, was to do legal work in London, either as a solicitor or barrister. In 1891 he thought of obtaining admission to the Inner Temple and obtained particulars of the cost. He also obtained information about the examinations he would have to pass before he could be called. The efforts to make a living from legal work in London came to nothing, and the following is typical of several letters William received from his brother at this period:

I haven't got any cash. Will you bring me £10 with you to-morrow *without fail* or I shall be in a dickens of a pickle. I hope to be able before the recess to make London pay for itself.

Lloyd George's next idea to raise cash was by getting Samuel Storey, the well-to-do Liberal M.P. for Sunderland, interested in providing the lion's share of the capital to buy the *Herald* newspapers of Caernarfon. Quite apart from the income directorates the new company might provide for the two brothers, control of the company would secure a favourable press for Lloyd George politically. He was always aware of the importance to a politician of having a well-disposed press on whose support he could rely. He wrote urgent letters to his brother asking him to help him with the negotiations. In May 1891 he wrote:

My dear W.

Herald

This is the present position of the matter. The *Genedl* will sell for probably £3,000 and the *Herald* for £7 to £8,000, i.e. whole concern
174

for £11,000. Of this the *Genedl* are willing to take their proportion in shares. But the *Herald* will only take £1,500, thus leaving us to find £6,500 ourselves. Here comes the rub. Our M.Ps. won't take much more than £1,000 between them. Now where are we to find the balance? You can't appeal to the investing public in N. Wales until your company is floated. The *Herald* must be assured the *cash* before it agrees to sell.

Well at last I have got hold of an old chap, who is willing to finance the thing, i.e. he'll find the cash. Mr. Storey, M.P. for Sunderland, an old hand at these things says he'll find the capital. . . . We would then with Storey's help buy at say £11,000, spend another £2,000 in improved machinery and then put the thing on the market at say £15,000. That's the idea. This transaction ought to pay. I shall charge professionally in any event.

Dy frawd, [thy brother] D.

When William George wrote to Lloyd George on 13 May 1891, he did not even mention this proposal. He told him (in Welsh) that in the year since his election, he hadn't done much, and asked—'Why don't you take part in this Irish debate?' The idea of making £2,000 profit out of Storey's capital was really too much of a pipe-dream for William George to have taken it seriously. He knew exactly where he stood, and was even prepared to stay single so as not to involve himself in any commitments beyond those he had already shouldered on behalf of his mother, uncle, unmarried sister—and now his politican brother, whom, he believed, was destined for great things. Occasionally David Lloyd George would write William, half in jest, urging him to get married. This is what William George entered in his diary on 3 May 1891:

My idea on the subject of matrimony is simply this—whatever pleasure and gain matrimony would bring me, it would be bound to cause infinite grief and loss to those who love me and whom I honour and love. It is therefore my duty not to harbour any ideas of matrimony with anyone, be she ever so rich or virtuous.

Later that month William George was taken ill, and Lloyd George came down from London to take charge of the practice for a couple of weeks before returning to London. On 9 June David wrote to William:

Very glad to hear Maggie tell me that you stood your outing yesterday extremely well. . . . They all tell me here—Bryn Roberts, Ellis Griffith and Alfred Thomas that you should guard yourself the first few days you go out. Take care you don't work too hard. . . . So much in the way of reminding you of *your duty to yourself—a thing you are often too apt to forget.*

By the beginning of July William George was working as hard as ever, and on 4 July Richard Lloyd recorded that he lost the last train home from the office, and had to walk home. He arrived in the house about 11 p.m. William George seldom, if ever, complained in his diary about his lot. He did not bear any kind of resentment against David; on the contrary, he wrote him cheerful letters (with the cash), which Lloyd George said made Maggie and him laugh, often uncontrollably.

Excessive hard work was not the only thing William George had to put up with; he sometimes had to suffer 'an illegitimate peering into his correspondence' by his mother, such was her apprehension that William George might leave her. On another occasion he was lectured by Richard Lloyd over some trifling matters after he'd returned from the office. When his Uncle Lloyd invaded the privacy of his bedroom at ten o'clock when he'd been at it all day, ticking him off for not reading some note he'd made, William George told him to leave the room, and commented that Richard Lloyd was 'deplorably deficient in human nature and common sense to act in the way he does'.

William George, submitting to conditions which most would have found intolerable, did not regard Lloyd George's relentless pursuit of his political career as an unjust imposition inflicted on him by fate. He was able to a surprising degree, under his crushing load of office and family responsibilities, to share vicariously in Lloyd George's political progress, giving him advice as to the content of his speeches and the climate of opinion in Wales on issues of the day—particularly in the constituency of the Caernarfon Boroughs. With only a narrow majority of eighteen to sustain him, both brothers knew how essential it was to broaden and strengthen the Liberal vote in the constituency before the 1892 General Election. If Lloyd George were to become a great social reformer, William George realized that he must encourage him to speak in meetings outside his own constituency, particularly in South Wales and the north of England. Within six months of his election in April 1890 Lloyd George had become a politician whose presence was frequently sought on public platforms the length and breadth of the land. William George's diary entry for 1 October 1890 read:

David came down soon after I had taken my tea. We went out together. I had full particulars of the St. Helen's meeting and trip. When one thinks of it, the progress D. has made is something wonderful, and John Morley's compliment—'The very brilliant speech of my young colleague'—will undoubtedly set him spinning along at a still faster rate. God speed him, say I. But what will become of me? I think that I also am acquiring a mint of moral force, and that one day I shall be able to and will score something for Jesus Christ. I am becoming more and more convinced that what I ought to aim at is to become a truly good man.

Lloyd George had written to William George to secure his agreement that he should attend the St. Helen's meeting. In his letter, giving his consent, he told Lloyd George of the suicide of a Porthmadog miller. Lloyd George's reply revealed how far he had, by October 1890, travelled on the road away from the orthodoxy in which he had been brought up:

The Steam Mills affair is a deplorably sad one. I am not so sure that he did do the right thing after all. He knew that he had not the necessary business capacity that would enable him to combat with his difficulties, and his poor bereaved wife and family are likely to profit more by their sorrow than they would by his assistance. He calculated rightly and he would have been a coward not to have done the deed. Suicide is to my mind a perfectly justifiable escape out of difficulties and anguish. Seneca's philosophy is orthodoxy on this point.

When William George took stock at the end of 1890, this is what he entered in his diary:

In the few words I said in chapel on Christmas Eve I said that the history of this year had been a chequered one to most of us, full of light and shade. What makes this year particularly eventful in our history as a family is D.'s election to Parliament. So important has it been that it has to a great extent governed the course of my life for the rest of the year. During the election, of course, election work took up a great deal of my time and thought, and after it the continued absence of David from the office necessitated me making some changes in the routine of my life. It moreover threw me almost entirely on my own resources. Its effects are likely to be permanent. The conduct of a large business as ours now if for the twelve months requires any amount of pluck and self-reliance. The business has known no diminution since D. went away, but rather has gone on increasing. I thank God from the bottom of my heart for the strength he has given me to conduct such a demanding business as ours is. It is a very worrying and anxious business, all depending on energy, ability and character. I thank the Lord and take comfort.

William George was also helped by a strong, innate sense of humour, which he shared with his sister-in-law Margaret Lloyd

177

George. He had also a ready wit, which never deserted him. When the preacher at the first Sunday service he attended after his hundredth birthday asked him to choose a hymn, he at once replied: 'It can only be the Old Hundredth!' Lloyd George always recognized his brother's unfailing loyalty and the support he received from him, without which his political career during the years of the unpaid Member of Parliament would have been an unattainable ambition. On the passing of the Finance Act, 1910—the famous People's Budget—Lloyd George sent a bound copy to William George, inscribed:

To my brother with a deep appreciation of his devotion and self-sacrifice which enabled me to give so much time to my public work.
May 31, 1910   D. Lloyd George

The partnership of Lloyd George & George extended beyond the legal domain, and was in a sense the foundation of the welfare-state. For both brothers the road had been a difficult one but when I reflect on their achievement I am reminded of T. S. Eliot's lines from *The Waste Land*:

> *Who is the third who walks always beside you?*
> *When I count, there are only you and I together*
> *But when I look ahead up the white road*
> *There is always another one walking beside you. . . .*

INDEX

Acland, Arthur Dyke, M.P., 159, 160, 170
America: Civil War, 89, 171; emigration to, 26, 89

Baptists: Disciples of Christ, in Criccieth, 17, 26–7, in Porthmadog, 81; Scotch Baptists, in Llanystumdwy and Criccieth, 15, 16, 18, 19, 26, 28, in N. Wales, 34, in Pwllheli, 56
Battersea Teachers' Training Institute, 38, 40
Bible, 28, 57, 70, 130
Bishop, Judge, 129, 153–6
Blaenau (Blaina), Monmouthshire school, 52
Blaenau Ffestiniog, 80, 125, 129–31
Breese, Edward, solicitor, 78, 79, 80, 84–5, 86, 102
Breese, Jones & Casson, solicitors, 78, 84, 102, 103, 119, 134, 135, 146, 160
British Schools, 39–40, 45, 49, 52, 56, 72–5
Brown, Mrs., first wife of W. George senior, 50–1
Bullford, 63, 64, 65, 66

Caernarfon, 39, 69, 156, 157, 158, 161, 165, 167, 169, 170, 171
Campbell, Alexander, 26, 27
Casson, Randall, solicitor, 79, 87, 93, 97, 104, 105, 106, 118, 119, 121, 122, 123, 135
Chamberlain, Joseph, M.P., 111, 113, 126, 127, 128, 131, 132–3, 160

Chapels: in Criccieth, Capel Berea (Baptist), 116, 138; Capel Mawr (Methodist), 137, 147–8, 149; Capel Seion (Methodist), 137, 148; Capel Uchaf, Pen-y-maes (Baptist), 17, 18, 26, 28, 32, 33, 34, 57
Charles, Mary (later Mrs. D. George, then Mrs. B. Williams), 14, 36, 46, 53–4, 64
Church of England, 34, 72, 76–7, 91, 112, 152
Church of Rome, 54
Clay, Henry, 79, 100
Clifton, Harvey, London solicitor, 171, 173
Criccieth, D. Ll. Jones buried there, 62; George family move to live in, 83, 96; political meetings at, 92, 129; Fair Day, 109, 152; Debating Society in, 124, 125–6; D. Ll. George's practice in, 134; home of Margaret Owen, 137; scene of her courting, 136–50; celebrates D. Ll. George's marriage, 150; Parliamentary Borough, 156; celebrates D. Ll. George's election, 170; see also Chapels

Daniel, David Robert, 157
Davitt, Michael, 113, 125, 129–31, 151
Dillwyn, L. Llewelyn, M.P., 162–3
Disestablishment of the Church in Wales, 124, 152, 158, 162–3, 165, 166, 169
Dwyfor and Dwyfach, rivers, 25, 30–1, 97

179